277 SHOCKING WORLD WAR II FACTS

The Ultimate Collection of Incredible WWII Stories, Hidden History, and Trivia Facts

---

SCOTT MATTHEWS

The more that you read, the more things you will know. The more you learn, the more places you'll go.

- Dr. Seuss

Contents

WORLD WAR II

Sep 1931
Japan Invades Manchuria

Sep 1939
Germany Invades Poland

Sep 1939
Britain and France Declare War on Germany

Dec 1941
Japan Attacks Pearl Harbor

Aug 1942–Feb 1943
Battle of Stalingrad

Oct-Nov 1942
Battle of El Alamein

Jun 6, 1944
D-Day: Allied Invasion of France

Dec 1944–Jan 1945
Battle of the Bulge

Apr-May 1945
Battle of Berlin

May 8, 1945
Germany Surrenders (V-E Day)

Introduction

In the early decades of the twentieth century, much of the world believed it was moving steadily toward stability and modernity. Cities expanded upward and outward. Radio signals crossed oceans. Passenger planes shrank continents. Electricity illuminated streets that had once gone dark at sunset. Medicine advanced, and factories multiplied. International trade tied distant economies together.

To many observers, the devastation of World War I had taught humanity a lasting lesson. The scale of that catastrophe, its slaughter, starvation, and shattered empires, seemed so extreme that surely no nation would willingly plunge into something similar again. Diplomacy, global institutions, and economic interdependence were supposed to prevent another such collapse.

They were wrong.

Beneath the outward appearance of recovery and progress, the world remained tense and uncertain. Many people were unhappy with the peace settlements that had followed World War I, and long-standing disputes over territory continued to cause friction between nations. Economic problems, including inflation, widespread unemployment, and heavy national debts, placed enormous strain on societies across the globe. At the same time, extreme political movements gained influence by offering clear promises of renewal and strength during periods of fear and instability.

Governments responded to these pressures by investing heavily in new armies, air forces, and naval fleets, believing that military power was the best way to protect their interests. Strategic planners worked carefully on invasion schedules and mobilization plans that were organized down to precise timetables. International alliances grew more rigid, binding countries together in ways that left little room for compromise, while propaganda campaigns increasingly shaped public opinion and fueled hostility toward rival states.

The international system appeared stable on the surface, but in reality, it was fragile and easily disturbed. Only a small increase in tension was needed to push it toward open conflict.

During the 1930s, that pressure mounted. Territory was seized. Treaties were ignored. Smaller nations vanished from maps. Each move was justified as necessary, temporary, or defensive. Each made the next crisis more dangerous. By the end of the decade, the world was standing at the edge of another catastrophe.

When war finally erupted, it didn't remain local for long. Within months, armies were crossing borders on multiple continents. Cities burned under aerial bombardment. Shipping lanes became killing grounds. Civilians found themselves drafted into the struggle, whether they wore uniforms or not.

What followed wasn't merely a continuation of earlier conflicts: it was warfare on a scale never before attempted.

World War II became the most destructive confrontation in human history. It fused ideology, industry, science, and nationalism into a single, relentless machine. Large formations of tanks advanced across continents, submarines hunted shipping lanes beneath the oceans, and bomber fleets carried the war deep into civilian areas. Rockets crossed national borders, while scientists in secret laboratories worked urgently to develop weapons powerful enough to destroy entire cities in moments.

The battlefield expanded everywhere: deserts, jungles, frozen plains, crowded ports, remote islands, and capital streets. Soldiers endured exhaustion, terror, and conditions that tested the limits of survival. Civilians rationed food, built shelters, evacuated children, labored in factories, and learned to live under constant threat from the air. Occupied populations navigated fear, collaboration, and resistance. Prisoners marched, starved, and died in staggering numbers.

When the fighting finally stopped, the toll defied comprehension. Tens of millions were dead. Entire regions lay in ruins. Cities had been flattened. Communities erased. Trauma followed survivors for decades. New political orders emerged from the wreckage, reshaping international relations, borders, and power structures for generations to come.

The world that followed wasn't simply rebuilt; it was transformed.

This book is not a conventional chronological textbook. It does not attempt to narrate every campaign in detail or catalogue every general and treaty. Instead, it approaches the war through moments: striking, unsettling, revealing details that illuminate what this global catastrophe truly looked like from the ground, the cockpit, the factory floor, the laboratory, and the living room.

Inside these pages, you will encounter:

The strange episodes.

The brutal realities.

The overlooked details.

The astonishing improvisations.

The human decisions that bent history in unexpected directions.

You will read about soldiers and spies, engineers and nurses, prisoners and pilots, factory workers and children. About inventions born of desperation. About accidents that altered campaigns. About acts of courage that went unnoticed and mistakes whose consequences echoed for decades.

Some of these facts will surprise you.

Some will disturb you.

Some may change how you think about modern warfare entirely.

Each stands alone, yet together they form a mosaic of a conflict that reshaped the planet and continues to influence politics, technology, and culture today. This is not only the story of how World War II unfolded. It is a collection of moments showing what happens when ideology, fear, ambition, and industrial power collide on a global scale.

This is *Shocking World War II Facts*.

ONE

A War That Engulfed the World

World War II is often remembered through its most famous battles and turning points, but the reality is that the conflict reached nearly every corner of the globe. From the cities of Europe to the deserts of North Africa, from the jungles of Southeast Asia to the vast expanses of the Pacific Ocean, the war drew in nations, colonies, and peoples on an unprecedented scale. Millions of individuals who had little influence over political decisions found themselves caught in a struggle that crossed borders and continents. This chapter explores the truly global nature of World War II, including the spread of conflict across multiple theaters, the involvement of colonial forces, and the ways in which the war reshaped regions far beyond Europe. It reveals how interconnected the world had become and how a crisis in one part of the globe could rapidly expand into a worldwide confrontation. It was a war that did not remain confined to a single front but instead transformed into a conflict that affected the entire world in ways that are still felt today.

1. Manchuria as an Early Spark

In September 1931, Japan set in motion one of the earliest crises that later blended into World War II when its forces moved into Manchuria, a resource-rich area of northeastern China. Japanese officers used an explosion along a railway near the Japanese-occupied city of Mukden, an incident whose circumstances were immediately disputed, as justification for a rapid military occupation. Within months, large areas of territory were under Japanese control, and a new puppet regime was installed to legitimize the takeover. At the time, this didn't look like the beginning of a world-spanning conflict; to many governments, it appeared to be another regional war in a turbulent post-World War I landscape. Yet in hindsight, historians often treat Manchuria as one of the first cracks in the fragile international order, a sign that armed expansion could succeed even in an age supposedly governed by diplomacy.

2. International Protests and a Quiet Departure

The reaction to Japan's move into Manchuria revealed how weak global enforcement mechanisms had become during the interwar years. China appealed to the League of Nations, an organization established after World War I to prevent future conflicts through diplomacy and collective security. The League of Nations sent investigators and eventually condemned the occupation. Japan rejected the criticism, also known as the Lytton Report, and, rather than reverse course, withdrew from the League entirely in 1933, signaling that it no longer felt bound by that system of collective security. This episode mattered far beyond East Asia. Other governments watched closely and drew their own conclusions about how much resistance territorial expansion might provoke. The Manchurian crisis didn't yet ignite a global war, but it demonstrated that treaties and international pressure alone were proving insufficient to stop determined states: an unsettling precedent as the 1930s continued to unfold.

3. Ethiopia and the Limits of Collective Security

In October 1935, Italy launched a full-scale invasion of Ethiopia, then commonly called Abyssinia, turning another regional crisis into a test of the international system meant to preserve peace. Under the leadership of Benito Mussolini, Italian forces advanced from neighboring colonies using modern weapons against a largely under-equipped defender. The government in Addis Ababa appealed again to the League of Nations, which imposed economic sanctions on Italy but avoided measures that might provoke war, such as cutting off vital oil supplies. Those limited penalties failed to halt the invasion, and by 1936, Ethiopia had been conquered and absorbed into a new Italian empire in East Africa. To many observers, the episode was unsettling proof that aggressive expansion could succeed even when openly condemned, further weakening confidence in diplomatic institutions and encouraging other powers to test how far they might go.

4. Spanish Civil War

When civil war erupted in Spain in 1936, it quickly became more than an internal struggle; it became a "clash of ideologies" that divided the world. The conflict was fought between two main groups: the Republicans, who supported the country's democratically elected government, and the Nationalists, a rebel group of conservative military officers led by General Francisco Franco. The struggle drew in outside powers eager to shape Europe's political direction and to use Spain as a military laboratory. Germany and Italy supported Franco's Nationalists, seeing an opportunity to install a fellow fascist-style dictator in Western Europe. Meanwhile, the Soviet Union sent aid to the Republicans. Because major democracies like Britain and the U.S. remained officially neutral, thousands of private citizens from around the world, known as the International Brigades, traveled to Spain to fight against the spread of fascism. Fascism is a far-right political system characterized by dictatorial power, extreme nationalism, and the forceful suppression of any opposition. The war reached a horrific peak with the 1937 bombing of Guernica, a chilling preview of how civilian populations would be targeted from the air in the coming years.

5. China Drawn into Full-Scale War

In July 1937, fighting flared between Japanese and Chinese troops near the Marco Polo Bridge outside Beijing, turning years of tension into open conflict between Japan and China. What began as a confused nighttime confrontation over troop movements quickly escalated into a massive invasion. This escalation forced the Chinese government, led by Generalissimo Chiang Kai-shek, the head of the Nationalist Party (Kuomintang) and the country's military leader, to abandon his previous policy of cautious compromise and mobilize for a "war of resistance." As Japanese forces captured major coastal cities, Chiang Kai-shek relocated his government deep inland to the mountain city of Chongqing, vowing to wear down the invaders through a prolonged struggle of attrition. The conflict was marked by devastating air raids and atrocities that shocked the international community, yet Chiang Kai-shek's forces remained the primary barrier to total Japanese control of the mainland. Although often viewed abroad as a separate Asian conflict, this war tied down millions of Japanese troops and reshaped global diplomacy. When Europe eventually descended into war in 1939, the fighting in China didn't pause; under Chiang's continued leadership, it merged into the broader Allied effort: the collective military struggle of the "Allied Powers," an alliance of nations including Great Britain, the Soviet Union, and eventually the United States, who united to defeat the aggression of the Axis powers (Germany, Italy, and Japan).

6. Appeasement and Territorial Gambles

While Asia burned, Europe moved closer to crisis through a series of calculated risks and hesitant responses driven by the ambitions of Adolf Hitler, the leader of the Nazi Party, who had risen to power in Germany with a promise to undo the "humiliations" of World War I. In 1936, Hitler ordered German troops to march back into the Rhineland, a strategically vital strip of German land bordering France that had been strictly demilitarized by international treaty to act as a safety buffer. Though this was a blatant violation of post-war agreements, it met no military resistance. Two years later, Germany absorbed Austria and then pressed claims on parts of Czechoslovakia. Britain and France, desperate to avoid another continent-wide slaughter, pursued a policy known as appeasement: negotiation rather than confrontation. This culminated in the Munich Agreement of 1938, which handed over disputed Czech territory to Germany in exchange for Hitler's promises of peace. While many celebrated the deal as a triumph for diplomacy, the victory was short-lived. Within months, German forces occupied the rest of Czechoslovakia, making it increasingly clear that Hitler's goals weren't limited to reclaiming lost territory but were aimed at total European dominance.

7. A Border War in the Mongolian Region

In the summer of 1939, fighting erupted far from Europe along the remote frontier between Mongolia and Japanese-controlled territory in Manchuria, near the Khalkhin Gol River. Forces from Japan clashed repeatedly with Mongolian troops backed by the Soviet Union (USSR), a vast communist state led by Joseph Stalin that spanned Eurasia and sought to protect its eastern borders from Japanese expansion. In August and September, Soviet armored units and artillery, coordinated with air power under the command of future war hero Georgy Zhukov, eventually encircled and crushed major Japanese formations. The defeat was costly for Tokyo and carried consequences well beyond the battlefield. Japanese leaders quietly abandoned plans for further northern expansion into Siberia and instead shifted attention southward toward Southeast Asia and the Pacific, a strategic decision that would later shape the course of the wider war.

Though largely overshadowed by events in Europe, Khalkhin Gol was a turning point in Asia before the global conflict formally ignited.

8. A Pact That Shocked Europe

As tensions mounted across Europe in 1939, diplomacy produced one of the most shocking agreements in history: a non-aggression pact between Nazi Germany and the Soviet Union. On the surface, the two countries, led by Adolf Hitler and Joseph Stalin, publicly promised not to attack one another. This stunned the world because the two leaders were bitter ideological enemies; Hitler's fascism and Stalin's communism were completely opposed. However, the treaty contained secret clauses that weren't revealed to the public. In these hidden terms, the two dictators agreed to carve up Eastern Europe between them. They planned to invade and divide Poland and decided that the Baltic states (Estonia, Latvia, and Lithuania) would fall under Soviet control. This deal was a strategic "win" for both dictators and served as the final green light for global conflict. For Germany, it meant that Hitler could invade Poland without the fear of the Soviet Union attacking him from the east, allowing him to focus his military strength in one direction. For the Soviet Union, the agreement bought Stalin vital time to build up his military and established a "buffer zone" of occupied territory in Eastern Europe to keep any future German threats far from the Soviet heartland. The signing of this pact was the final green light for war. With his eastern border secured by this temporary friendship, Hitler was ready to launch his invasion.

9. The Attack That Opened the European War

In the early hours of September 1, 1939, German forces crossed into Poland, launching a coordinated assault that many historians treat as the formal beginning of World War II in Europe. Armored columns advanced along multiple fronts while aircraft struck railways, bridges, and cities, aiming to paralyze Polish defenses before they could fully mobilize. German propaganda claimed the invasion was defensive, but the operation followed months of planning and was made politically possible by the recent non-aggression pact with the Soviet Union. Polish troops resisted fiercely, but they were outmatched in equipment and air support. Within days, refugees clogged roads and rail lines, governments across Europe rushed to emergency meetings, and it became clear that the diplomatic crises of the 1930s had finally tipped into open continental war.

10. Declarations That Globalized a Conflict

Germany's invasion of Poland forced other powers to decide whether years of warnings and guarantees would finally be backed by action. On September 3, 1939, the United Kingdom and France formally declared war on Germany after ultimatums demanding withdrawal from Poland went unanswered. The announcements were brief and legalistic, but their implications were enormous: what had begun as a regional invasion was now a war between Europe's major powers. Crowds gathered around radios in cities and villages, soldiers were mobilized, and navies began positioning themselves across the Atlantic and Mediterranean. Although little immediate fighting followed on the Western Front, the diplomatic threshold had been crossed. The long sequence of crises stretching back to Manchuria and Ethiopia had culminated in a confrontation that now threatened to spread far beyond Poland's borders.

11. A Second Army from the East

As Polish forces struggled to slow the German advance in September 1939, another blow arrived from an unexpected direction. On September 17, troops from the Soviet Union crossed Poland's eastern frontier, acting under the secret provisions of the recent German–Soviet agreement. Soviet officials claimed that the Polish state had collapsed and that they were moving in to protect local populations, but the action effectively sealed Poland's defeat. Already stretched thin, Polish units found themselves facing two invading powers at once, while political leaders fled abroad to continue resistance in exile. Within weeks, the country was divided between its occupiers, and millions of civilians came under new, often brutal administrations. The double invasion shocked observers abroad and confirmed that the European war was no longer limited to a single aggressor but was already reshaping the balance of power across the continent.

12. Finland's Winter Struggle

Only months later, another front opened in the north when the Soviet Union attacked Finland in November 1939 after negotiations over territory and security guarantees broke down. Expecting a swift victory, Soviet planners instead encountered fierce resistance from Finnish troops who used skis, camouflage, and intimate knowledge of forests and frozen lakes to offset overwhelming numbers. Fighting took place in temperatures that plunged far below zero, with weapons freezing and soldiers suffering severe frostbite alongside combat wounds. Although Finland was eventually forced to cede territory in March 1940, it preserved its independence and inflicted unexpectedly heavy losses on the invaders. The campaign drew international attention, exposed weaknesses in Soviet military preparedness, and demonstrated how the war was already spreading into new and unforgiving environments only months after it began.

13. Denmark's Sudden Fall

In April 1940, Germany abruptly expanded the war northward by attacking Denmark, seeking to secure supply routes for Swedish iron ore, a high-quality mineral essential for the production of German steel, tanks, and ships. Because Germany lacked sufficient domestic resources, these shipments from neutral Sweden were the lifeblood of its war machine. The German assault also aimed to block any future presence of the Allied Powers: the international coalition led by Britain and France that had formed in September 1939 to oppose German aggression. The assault came with almost no warning. German troops crossed the border at dawn while aircraft flew low over Copenhagen, dropping leaflets urging surrender rather than resistance. Denmark's small and lightly equipped military faced an overwhelming force, and government leaders feared that continued fighting would lead to the destruction of cities and civilian casualties. After only a few hours of combat, Danish authorities agreed to surrender, making it one of the fastest national defeats of the entire war. Strategically, the occupation gave Germany control of airfields, ports, and sea lanes into the Baltic Sea, a large body of water in Northern Europe that is nearly enclosed by land, serving as the primary maritime highway connecting Germany, Scandinavia, and the Soviet Union. By controlling Denmark, Germany effectively locked the "gate" to this sea, signaling to Europe that the conflict was spreading into new regions vital for resources and transportation.

14. Norway's Fjords and Frozen Battles

On the same day as the Danish operation, German forces struck Norway, whose long coastline and deep fjords, which are long, narrow inlets with steep cliffs or slopes created by glaciers that reach far inland, made it crucial for Atlantic naval access. These natural harbors provided ideal hiding spots for warships and were vital for protecting the iron ore shipments coming from Sweden. Unlike Denmark, Norway resisted, and British and French units soon landed to support its defense. Fighting erupted around ports, mountain passes, and snowbound roads, while warships clashed offshore and paratroopers seized key airfields inland. For weeks, the campaign remained uncertain, but Germany steadily poured in reinforcements by sea and air. By early June 1940, Allied troops withdrew, and Norwegian authorities fled into exile, leaving the country under occupation. The campaign gave Germany valuable submarine bases along the Atlantic coast and demonstrated how air power, speed, and control of infrastructure could overcome difficult terrain in modern warfare.

15. Overrunning of France in Weeks

In May 1940, the conflict in Western Europe reached a stunning climax when German armies surged through Belgium, the Netherlands, and Luxembourg before driving into France itself. Allied commanders expected the main thrust to follow heavily fortified borders, but German armored divisions instead cut through the Ardennes, a densely forested region long believed to be unsuitable for tanks. This surprise maneuver split the defending forces and triggered a massive civilian flight, as roads filled with millions of refugees. Within just a few weeks, German troops reached the English Channel coast, Paris fell, and French leaders were forced to request an armistice. By June 1940, the French surrender was official. The speed of the collapse shocked the world and completely overturned long-held assumptions about defensive warfare, leaving Britain isolated in Western Europe and marking one of the most dramatic turning points of the early war.

16. Trapping of Allied Forces

In mid-May 1940, German armored spearheads, fast-moving groups of tanks and motorized vehicles designed to punch a hole through enemy lines and race deep into the rear, tore through northern France and Belgium. This "lightning" maneuver cut off large Allied armies from the south, forcing British and French units to retreat toward the port city of Dunkirk. Located on the coast of the English Channel near the Belgian border, Dunkirk sat roughly forty-seven miles (seventy-five kilometers) from the British coast. The town's beaches and harbor became the final escape route for soldiers surrounded by advancing German troops on land and attacked by the Luftwaffe (the German air force) from the sky.

17. Encirclement on the Channel Coast

By May 24, 1940, nearly 400,000 Allied soldiers from the United Kingdom and France were crowded into sand dunes, narrow streets, and improvised defensive lines around the port city of Dunkirk. German forces closed in from land while aircraft bombed harbor facilities, destroying docks and blocking many large ships from approaching. Thousands of men were forced to wait for days in the open, exposed to strafing attacks and artillery fire, wading into cold water in hopes of reaching rescue vessels offshore. Many feared that the capture of the entire British Expeditionary Force was unavoidable. What looked like the destruction of Britain's army in Western Europe was instead becoming a desperate race against time, as commanders scrambled to assemble any vessel capable of crossing the Channel.

18. Operation Dynamo and the Little Ships

The crisis at Dunkirk triggered a dramatic rescue effort beginning on May 26, 1940, when British naval planners launched an emergency evacuation code-named Operation Dynamo. Coordinated from headquarters in southern England, the plan relied not only on warships but also on hundreds of civilian craft pressed into service, fishing trawlers, ferries, tugboats, pleasure boats, and river launches, many of them crewed by volunteers. These small vessels ferried troops from shallow beaches to destroyers and transports waiting farther offshore while German aircraft attacked relentlessly from above. Smoke from burning fuel tanks drifted across the coast, and wrecked ships littered the harbor approaches. By the time the operation ended on June 4, roughly 338,000 Allied soldiers had been carried to safety, though nearly all heavy equipment had been left behind. The evacuation transformed a looming catastrophe into a defining moment of wartime survival and ensured Britain could continue fighting.

19. Attacks Across the Channel

After the fall of France in June 1940, Germany turned its focus toward forcing the United Kingdom out of the war. Beginning in July, the German air force launched sustained strikes against merchant shipping in the English Channel and radar installations along Britain's southern coastline. These tall towers, using radio waves to detect approaching aircraft, formed an early-warning shield that allowed defenders precious minutes to prepare. The attacks were intended to weaken Britain's ability to respond in the air and to clear the way for a planned cross-Channel invasion known as Operation Sea Lion. At first, the campaign focused on infrastructure rather than cities, signaling that Germany hoped to defeat Britain militarily before risking a costly amphibious landing.

20. Britain's Integrated Air Defense System

To counter the growing air threat, Britain relied on a carefully coordinated defensive network unlike anything previously attempted on such a scale. Radar stations, coastal observers, and command centers were linked by telephone lines and plotting rooms that tracked enemy formations in real time. Instead of keeping fighters circling endlessly in the sky, controllers directed squadrons to take off only when needed, conserving fuel and allowing pilots to meet raids at optimal altitudes. German bombers and escort fighters repeatedly struck airfields in counties closest to France, such as Kent and Sussex, hoping to cripple this system and destroy defending aircraft on the ground. The struggle soon became one of endurance and organization as much as raw firepower, with each side testing whether technology, logistics, and coordination could decide control of the skies before an invasion was attempted.

21. Pilots from Many Nations

The aerial defense of Britain depended heavily on young fighter pilots who flew exhausting schedules, sometimes scrambling into combat several times a day. While many were British, hundreds came from countries already under Axis occupation: nations conquered by the "Axis Powers," the military alliance led by Nazi Germany, Fascist Italy, and later Imperial Japan. These pilots included skilled airmen from Poland and Czechoslovakia who had escaped their homelands to continue the fight. They were joined by volunteers from Commonwealth nations, a global association of countries that were formerly part of the British Empire, such as Canada, Australia, and New Zealand, which shared a common allegiance to the British Crown. These volunteers brought valuable combat experience and formed some of the most effective units of the campaign. Air battles erupted daily above farmland, seaside towns, and crowded suburbs, turning ordinary landscapes into contested airspace. Losses mounted on both sides, and replacement pilots were rushed through training to keep squadrons operational. By August 1940, the fighting had hardened into a grinding contest of attrition: a tactical struggle where each side attempted to wear down the other's resources and personnel. The survival of the country became increasingly dependent on whether its air defenses could remain intact longer than those of its opponent.

22. Night Raids over London

In September 1940, German strategy shifted away from airfields toward sustained bombing of major population centers, especially London. These nighttime assaults, later known collectively as the Blitz, dropped high-explosive bombs and incendiaries that ignited widespread fires, flattened neighborhoods, and forced civilians into underground stations and public shelters. Other industrial cities were also struck repeatedly as ports, factories, and rail yards burned. The campaign continued through the winter and into the spring of 1941, yet aircraft production and air defenses remained active despite the destruction. Public morale, though shaken, didn't collapse. By October, German leaders postponed plans for an invasion indefinitely, marking the first major strategic failure of their westward expansion and ensuring that the war in Europe would continue rather than end swiftly in the air.

23. Submarines in the Supply Lines

As Britain resisted invasion in 1940, Germany intensified a campaign at sea designed to starve the United Kingdom into submission. German submarines, called U-boats, short for the German word *Unterseeboot*, meaning "undersea boat," slipped into the Atlantic shipping lanes to attack merchant vessels carrying food, fuel, and weapons from North America. These ships usually traveled in convoys, tightly grouped formations meant to make defense easier, but early in the war, many lacked sufficient escort warships or air cover. U-boats often attacked at night on the surface, firing torpedoes and vanishing into darkness before counterattacks could begin. Sinkings mounted rapidly, alarming British planners who understood that losing cargo ships faster than they could be replaced threatened the nation's ability to survive the war at all.

24. Escorts, Sonar, and Closing the Ocean Gaps

Britain and its allies gradually learned how to fight back against the submarine menace. Warships were equipped with sonar, an underwater detection system that used sound waves to locate submerged vessels, and depth charges, explosive barrels dropped into the sea to damage or destroy submarines below. Aircraft began patrolling shipping routes as well, forcing U-boats to dive and slowing their attacks. Long stretches of ocean that aircraft couldn't yet reach, known as the "air gap," proved especially dangerous until longer-range planes and escort carriers were introduced. Convoy systems were tightened, and intelligence efforts tracked German naval communications. The campaign became a battle of production as much as tactics: Germany rushed to build more submarines, while Britain and the United States expanded shipyards to replace lost vessels faster than they could be sunk. Control of the Atlantic would become one of the war's decisive struggles.

25. A New Front in the Mediterranean

In June 1940, Italy entered the conflict on Germany's side, opening new fronts around the Mediterranean Sea and in North Africa. Italian forces advanced from Libya into British-controlled Egypt, aiming to threaten the Suez Canal, a vital man-made waterway that served as a shortcut for ships traveling between Europe and the "colonies" (territories ruled by distant nations) in Asia and East Africa. For Britain, losing the canal would mean losing its quickest access to the resources of its global empire and the critical oil supplies of the Middle East. Early fighting revealed major problems with Italian equipment, coordination, and long supply lines stretching across the harsh, trackless desert terrain. British counteroffensives, aided by troops from across the British Empire, including India and Australia, soon pushed Italian units back, capturing large numbers of prisoners and alarming the leadership in Rome. Naval clashes and air raids spread across the Mediterranean as both sides tried to protect convoys, organized groups of merchant ships protected by warships, carrying fuel, food, and ammunition to distant armies. What had begun as a European war was now clearly spilling into the deserts and sea routes that connected three continents, turning the Mediterranean into a high-stakes battleground for global survival.

26. Rommel and the Desert See-Saw

To stabilize the collapsing Italian position, Germany sent an expeditionary force to North Africa in early 1941 under General Erwin Rommel. His units, known as the Afrika Korps, quickly launched bold counterattacks that drove British troops back across hundreds of miles of desert. The fighting became a mobile tug-of-war, with armored columns racing between isolated forts and supply depots while aircraft bombed roads and ports. Desert warfare placed enormous strain on logistics: vehicles consumed fuel at staggering rates, water was scarce, and spare parts had to be hauled over vast distances. Victories often depended less on battlefield brilliance than on whether one side could keep trucks, tanks, and troops supplied. The North African front soon turned into one of the war's most fluid and unpredictable theaters.

27. A Coup That Alarmed Berlin

In early 1941, Germany turned anxious attention toward Yugoslavia, a multi-ethnic state created after World War I that included Serbs, Croats, Slovenes, and several other South Slavic groups. The country's political balance suddenly collapsed when a coup overthrew a government that had recently aligned itself with the Axis. The change infuriated Adolf Hitler, who feared that instability in the Balkans could expose Germany's southern flank and disrupt crucial supply routes, especially those linked to Romanian oil fields. The episode convinced German leaders that Yugoslavia couldn't be left neutral or uncertain while larger military plans were underway. Within days, invasion orders were issued. What had looked like a regional political crisis quickly became the trigger for a new military campaign, one that would pull southeastern Europe directly into the widening war.

28. Blitzkrieg in Southeastern Europe

In April 1941, German and Italian forces launched simultaneous invasions of Yugoslavia and Greece, opening another major front only weeks before the planned assault on the Soviet Union. Heavy bombing struck cities, including the Yugoslav capital, Belgrade. Along with the bombing, armored columns and airborne troops crossed borders from multiple directions. Because attacks came at once from several sides, organized resistance collapsed rapidly. Within weeks, both countries were occupied or partitioned, carved into zones governed by different Axis powers and collaborators. The victories secured Germany's southern approaches, safeguarded supply routes near Romania, and extended Axis influence toward the eastern Mediterranean. Yet the campaigns also consumed precious weeks, delaying the much larger invasion of the Soviet Union that German planners were already preparing farther east.

29. Crete and the Age of Airborne Assaults

In May 1941, Germany attempted one of the most daring operations of the early war: the capture of the Mediterranean island of Crete almost entirely by parachute troops. The island, which had become an Allied stronghold after the fall of mainland Greece, controlled important sea routes and airfields. German paratroopers descended from transport planes under intense fire, suffering heavy casualties as defenders shot them while they were still landing and scrambling for their weapons. Fighting raged around villages and airstrips, and only after days of brutal combat did German forces secure enough runways to fly in reinforcements. Crete eventually fell, but at a staggering cost. The losses alarmed German commanders, who concluded that such large airborne invasions were too risky to repeat. The battle shaped later planning and revealed how experimental and costly modern warfare had become by 1941.

30. A Massive Army

Even as fighting continued around the Mediterranean, Germany quietly assembled enormous forces along the western border of the Soviet Union. At dawn on June 22, 1941, Adolf Hitler launched Operation Barbarossa, a vast invasion stretching hundreds of miles from the Baltic to the Black Sea. This attack was a profound act of betrayal, as it formally broke the Molotov-Ribbentrop Pact: the "non-aggression" agreement signed just two years earlier in which both nations had promised not to fight one another. The sudden strike caught the Soviet leadership by surprise, shattering the diplomatic peace that had allowed both dictators to carve up Eastern Europe in 1939. Three immense formations drove toward key objectives: Leningrad in the north, Moscow in the center, and Ukraine in the south. Aircraft smashed airfields and rail junctions, destroying hundreds of Soviet planes on the ground in the opening hours. German planners believed rapid armored thrusts and encirclement tactics would bring victory before winter. Instead, the invasion instantly transformed the war into a continental struggle of unprecedented scale across forests, rivers, and open land.

31. Encirclements and Catastrophic Losses

During the summer of 1941, German forces advanced deep into Soviet territory using mobile formations of tanks, trucks, and infantry to surround entire enemy armies in vast "pockets." Cities such as Minsk and Smolensk fell after fierce fighting, while hundreds of thousands of captured soldiers were marched westward under brutal conditions. The German policy toward prisoners proved especially lethal, with millions subjected to starvation, forced marches, and executions rather than being treated according to international norms. Civilians fled burning towns as front lines swept east, and destruction spread across enormous swaths of countryside. Although the German advance appeared unstoppable in its early months, the sheer distances involved, growing casualties, and stubborn Soviet resistance hinted that the campaign was becoming something far larger and far more dangerous than its planners had anticipated.

32. Encirclement of a Northern Metropolis

By September 1941, German and allied forces had reached the outskirts of Leningrad, today known as St. Petersburg, cutting most overland routes into the city and beginning what would become one of the longest sieges in modern warfare. Instead of launching an immediate frontal assault, German commanders chose to surround the metropolis and bombard key infrastructure, hoping that hunger, cold, and isolation would force surrender without the cost of street fighting. Rail links were severed, warehouses destroyed, and utilities disrupted as shells and bombs fell across residential districts. Millions of civilians, along with soldiers and factory workers producing weapons inside the city, suddenly found themselves trapped behind tightening lines. The encirclement turned daily survival into a strategic issue and marked the opening phase of a blockade that would last far longer and prove much deadlier than most observers initially expected.

33. Starvation and the Frozen Escape Route

As winter set in during late 1941, conditions inside besieged Leningrad deteriorated rapidly. Food rations dropped to only a few hundred calories a day, and tens of thousands of people died each month from hunger and exposure. The city's main lifeline ran across Lake Ladoga, where trucks and sled convoys crossed the frozen surface during winter in a hazardous supply route later called the "Road of Life." These journeys took place under constant artillery fire and air attack, and vehicles sometimes plunged through thin ice. Though never sufficient to fully relieve suffering, the route prevented complete collapse and allowed limited evacuations, turning a frozen lake into one of the war's most fragile and vital arteries.

34. The Final Push Toward Moscow

Farther south in autumn 1941, German forces renewed their drive toward Moscow, hoping that capturing the Soviet capital would cripple political leadership, transportation networks, and morale. Early advances brought forward units within sight of the city's outer suburbs, prompting emergency defensive measures and the evacuation of government offices eastward. Yet logistical problems mounted quickly. Seasonal rains transformed unpaved roads into deep mud, immobilizing tanks and trucks and slowing supply convoys. Rail lines struggled to keep pace with the rapidly shifting front, while exhausted troops fought in worsening weather. Soviet commanders rushed reinforcements into defensive belts surrounding the capital, digging trenches and fortifying villages in preparation for a last stand as temperatures plunged and the battle for central Russia entered a decisive phase.

35. Winter Counterblows in the East

By early December 1941, freezing temperatures and stretched supply lines had left German units around Moscow dangerously exposed. Many soldiers lacked adequate winter clothing, vehicles froze overnight, and fuel shortages slowed movement. Soviet forces, strengthened by newly deployed divisions and reorganized defenses, launched coordinated counterattacks along broad sections of the front. Ski troops played a critical role in this offensive: specialized mobile infantry units equipped with skis that allowed them to glide over deep snow that would trap a normal soldier, enabling them to launch surprise attacks from the forest. These ski troops and other mobile units exploited the frozen ground to strike German flanks and rear areas, pushing the invaders back dozens of miles from the capital. In some critical sectors, the Germans were forced to retreat as far as 150 miles (about 250 kilometers) away. The reversal shocked German commanders, who had expected the campaign to end months earlier. Although the fighting remained brutal, the counteroffensive marked the first major collapse of Germany's momentum in the east and demonstrated that the Soviet Union retained both the manpower and the will to continue a war that had already grown far beyond its planners' original expectations.

36. Rising Tensions in the Pacific

By late 1941, relations between Japan and the United States had deteriorated sharply. Japan had been fighting a prolonged war in China since 1937 and sought access to oil, rubber, and other raw materials in Southeast Asia to sustain its military expansion. In response, the United States and its allies imposed economic sanctions, including an embargo that cut off oil exports to Japan, resources essential for its navy and industry. Diplomatic negotiations continued throughout the year, but both sides prepared for the possibility of war. Japanese leaders faced a difficult choice: abandon expansionist goals or seize the resources they needed by force. As tensions rose, military planners began to consider a bold strategy that would attempt to disable American power in the Pacific before it could respond.

37. A Surprise Strike Across the Pacific

In late 1941, Japanese military planners prepared a high-risk operation designed to weaken the United States before it could interfere with expansion in Asia. The plan called for a long-range naval strike against the American Pacific Fleet stationed at Pearl Harbor, located on the island of Oahu in Hawaii, thousands of kilometers from Japan. Aircraft carriers, warships that carry and launch planes, would sail secretly across the northern Pacific, maintaining radio silence to avoid detection. The goal was to destroy battleships, aircraft, and fuel supplies in a single coordinated attack, buying Japan time to secure resource-rich territories in Southeast Asia. The strategy relied on complete surprise. If successful, it could delay the American response for months. If it failed, Japan risked provoking a powerful industrial nation into a prolonged war that it might not be able to win.

38. The Morning Attack

On the morning of December 7, 1941, Japanese aircraft launched their attack on Pearl Harbor in two waves, catching the base largely unprepared. Bombers and torpedo planes targeted battleships anchored in the harbor, while fighters strafed airfields to destroy American aircraft before they could take off. Within minutes, explosions tore through ships, including the battleship USS *Arizona*, which sank after a massive internal blast. Sailors scrambled to return fire as smoke and flames spread across the water. In total, more than 2,400 Americans were killed, and many ships were sunk or heavily damaged. However, key targets, including aircraft carriers, repair facilities, and fuel depots, remained intact, largely because they were absent or missed. Instead of securing a decisive advantage, the attack united American public opinion, leading to a formal declaration of war the following day.

39. Declarations of Global War

The attack on Pearl Harbor immediately transformed the conflict into a truly global war. On December 8, 1941, the United States formally declared war on Japan, marking a decisive shift in American policy after years of avoiding direct involvement. The following days widened the conflict even further. Japan's allies, Germany and Italy, declared war on the United States, bringing the world's largest industrial power into both the Pacific and European theaters simultaneously. What had previously been partially connected wars in Europe, Africa, and Asia now merged into a single, coordinated global struggle. Governments began to align their strategies, industries shifted to wartime production on an enormous scale, and millions of new soldiers were mobilized. The entry of the United States ensured that the war would expand not only geographically but also in resources, technology, and intensity.

40. Simultaneous Offensives Across the Pacific

In December 1941, immediately following the attack on Pearl Harbor, Japan launched a series of nearly simultaneous offensives across Southeast Asia and the Pacific. These attacks were carefully coordinated to strike multiple Allied positions at once, overwhelming defenders before they could organize an effective response. Japanese forces targeted British, American, and Dutch territories, focusing on key ports, airfields, and communication centers. The goal was to secure a defensive perimeter and gain access to vital natural resources such as oil, rubber, and minerals needed to sustain a long war. Because many Allied forces were unprepared or spread too thin, Japanese troops often achieved rapid successes. Within weeks, vast areas of territory had been captured, creating the impression that Japan's military expansion might be unstoppable.

41. The Fall of the Philippines

One of Japan's main objectives was the Philippines, a group of islands under American control that stood directly between Japan and Southeast Asia. Japanese aircraft struck airfields shortly after Pearl Harbor, destroying many planes on the ground and leaving defenses weakened. Ground forces soon landed and advanced toward the capital, Manila, forcing American and Filipino troops to retreat to the Bataan Peninsula. There, they held out for months under severe shortages of food, medicine, and supplies. When resistance finally collapsed in April 1942, tens of thousands of exhausted prisoners were forced to march long distances under brutal conditions in what became known as the Bataan Death March. The fall of the Philippines removed a major obstacle to Japanese expansion and demonstrated the harsh realities of captivity during the Pacific War.

42. Singapore and the Collapse of a Fortress

At the same time, Japanese forces advanced down the Malaya peninsula toward Singapore, a heavily fortified British naval base often described as the "Gibraltar of the East." British planners had expected any attack to come from the sea, but Japanese troops moved rapidly overland, using bicycles and light equipment to travel quickly through jungle terrain that defenders had considered difficult to cross. Air superiority allowed Japanese aircraft to strike supply lines and defensive positions, weakening resistance. By February 1942, Singapore was surrounded, and after a short but intense battle, British forces surrendered. More than 80,000 troops were taken prisoner, making it one of the largest defeats in British military history. The fall of Singapore shocked Allied governments and severely damaged confidence in colonial defenses across Asia.

43. Securing Oil in the Dutch East Indies

A key objective of Japanese expansion was control of the Dutch East Indies, a region rich in oil and other natural resources essential for modern warfare. Without reliable fuel supplies, Japan's navy, air force, and industry couldn't continue operating effectively. Japanese forces moved quickly to capture major oil fields and refineries, often encountering limited resistance as Allied defenses struggled to coordinate across vast distances. Naval battles were fought in surrounding seas, but Japanese fleets gained control, allowing transport ships to move troops and supplies with increasing security. By early 1942, most of the region had fallen under Japanese control, providing the resources needed to sustain further military operations. These victories gave Japan a temporary strategic advantage, but they also stretched its forces across a vast territory that would later become difficult to defend.

44. A Carrier Battle

In May 1942, opposing fleets met in the Coral Sea northeast of Australia in a battle that marked a new kind of naval warfare. For the first time, ships on both sides never directly saw each other; instead, aircraft launched from carriers searched for and attacked enemy vessels over long distances. Japan aimed to capture Port Moresby in New Guinea. Securing this port would have allowed Japan to dominate the region and threaten Australia's supply lines: the vital maritime routes used to transport food, fuel, military equipment, and fresh troops from the United States. If these lines had been cut, Australia would have been isolated, making it much harder for the Allies to launch a comeback in the Pacific. American and Australian forces moved to intercept the Japanese fleet. Over several days, both sides exchanged heavy air strikes, damaging or sinking major ships and losing dozens of aircraft. Although both sides suffered heavy losses, the Japanese advance toward Port Moresby was halted, marking their first major strategic setback of the Pacific war. The battle proved that aircraft carriers had replaced heavily armored battleships as the dominant force at sea. It demonstrated that in modern naval warfare, the side that controlled the air above the ocean would ultimately control the waves below.

45. The Turning Point at Midway

In June 1942, Japanese forces attacked Midway Atoll, expecting to draw out and destroy the remaining American carriers. Instead, they encountered a prepared defense. As Japanese aircraft rearmed on their carriers, American dive bombers arrived overhead, striking at a vulnerable moment. Within minutes, multiple Japanese carriers were set ablaze, their decks crowded with fuel and ammunition. The loss of these ships and their highly trained pilots was devastating. Japan could replace ships over time, but experienced aircrews were far harder to rebuild. The battle marked a major shift in the Pacific War, as Japan lost the ability to carry out large-scale offensive operations in the same way it had before.

46. From Expansion to Defense

After the Battle of Midway, Japan's rapid expansion slowed dramatically. Instead of advancing across the Pacific, Japanese troops were forced to defend a vast area of newly conquered territory stretching from Southeast Asia to remote island chains. Supply lines became longer and more difficult to protect, while Allied forces began planning counteroffensives. Control of key islands, airfields, and shipping routes became increasingly important as both sides prepared for prolonged conflict. The early phase of nearly uninterrupted Japanese victories had come to an end, replaced by a more balanced struggle in which industrial production, logistics, and long-term strategy would determine the outcome. The war had entered a new stage, where the initiative was beginning to shift.

47. Guadalcanal and the First Allied Offensive

In August 1942, Allied forces launched their first major offensive in the Pacific by landing on the island of Guadalcanal in the Solomon Islands chain. The island was strategically important because Japanese forces were building an airfield there that could threaten supply routes between the United States and Australia. American Marines landed and quickly captured the unfinished airstrip, later naming it Henderson Field. What followed were months of intense fighting on land, at sea, and in the air. Japanese forces launched repeated attempts to retake the island, often landing troops at night to avoid detection. Conditions were harsh, with heat, disease, and supply shortages affecting both sides. Guadalcanal marked a turning point because it shifted the initiative to the Allies, who were now beginning to move from defense to offense.

48. A War of Attrition in the Jungle

The campaign on Guadalcanal became a prolonged struggle of attrition, meaning a fight where each side attempts to wear the other down over time through continuous losses. Battles were fought in dense jungle, along narrow ridges, and around key positions such as Henderson Field. Night naval battles took place in nearby waters, where ships often engaged at close range in darkness. Both sides suffered heavy casualties not only from combat but also from malaria, malnutrition, and exhaustion. Supplies were difficult to deliver, and reinforcements often arrived under dangerous conditions. Japanese forces gradually weakened as their supply lines stretched too far, while American industrial capacity allowed a steady flow of replacements. By early 1943, Japan withdrew its remaining troops, marking its first major land defeat of the war and signaling a shift in momentum across the Pacific.

49. Expanding Across Multiple Fronts

By late 1942, World War II had become a truly global conflict, with major battles taking place simultaneously across Europe, North Africa, and the Pacific. In North Africa, Axis and Allied forces fought across deserts for control of strategic routes and resources. In the Soviet Union, massive armies clashed along an enormous front stretching thousands of miles. Meanwhile, in the Pacific, naval and island campaigns determined control of vast ocean regions. This multi-front war placed enormous demands on manpower, equipment, and logistics. Nations had to coordinate strategies across continents while maintaining supply lines that stretched across oceans and deserts. The scale of the conflict forced governments to mobilize entire societies, turning factories, farms, and civilian populations into essential parts of the war effort.

50. The Battle for Stalingrad Begins

In the summer of 1942, German forces launched a major offensive toward Stalingrad, a massive industrial city stretching along the banks of the Volga River in southern Russia. The city was a vital objective for two reasons: strategically, it was a major transport hub for moving fuel and grain from the south to the rest of the Soviet Union; and symbolically, capturing a city named after the Soviet leader, Joseph Stalin, would have been a devastating propaganda blow to Soviet morale. The German army, also known as the

Sixth Army, led by General Friedrich Paulus, advanced rapidly across the open steppe, aiming to seize the city. At the same time, other units drove further south toward the Caucasus, a region rich in oil fields that Hitler desperately needed to fuel his global war machine. By the time the Germans reached the outskirts of Stalingrad in August, the Luftwaffe (German air force) had reduced much of the city to rubble through intense firebombing. The conflict quickly devolved into a nightmare of urban warfare, or "Rattenkrieg" (Rat's War), as the Germans called it. Both sides committed millions of troops to the struggle, turning the city into a meat grinder. The battle was no longer just about territory; it became a test of wills that would eventually decide the future course of the war on the Eastern Front.

51. Street Fighting in Stalingrad

By late 1942, the battle for Stalingrad had turned into a brutal struggle fought at extremely close range. German and Soviet soldiers battled for control of factories, apartment blocks, and even individual rooms. The destruction was so extensive that rubble often became defensive positions, making it difficult for tanks and large units to maneuver. Fighting was constant, with snipers, machine guns, and grenades used in tight spaces. Soviet forces adopted a tactic of staying as close to German positions as possible, reducing the effectiveness of German artillery and air power. Civilians who remained in the city endured extreme conditions, sheltering in ruins while the fighting raged around them. The battle became a test of endurance, with both sides suffering heavy losses but neither willing to retreat.

52. Encirclement of the Sixth Army

In November 1942, Soviet forces launched a massive counteroffensive around Stalingrad, targeting the weaker Axis units guarding the flanks of the German army. These forces, which included Romanian and Hungarian troops, were less well equipped than the main German formations. The Soviet attack broke through their lines and advanced rapidly, linking up behind the city and surrounding the German Army. This maneuver, known as an encirclement, trapped more than 250,000 German and Allied soldiers inside Stalingrad. Cut off from supplies, they relied on limited air deliveries that proved insufficient to sustain them. As winter tightened its grip, the trapped forces faced severe shortages of food, fuel, and ammunition. What had begun as an offensive operation turned into a desperate struggle for survival.

53. Surrender in the Winter Cold

By early 1943, conditions inside the encircled German forces at Stalingrad had become unbearable. Starvation, freezing temperatures, and constant Soviet pressure weakened the trapped army. Attempts to break through the encirclement failed, and relief efforts from outside were unable to reach the city. Despite orders to hold their position, German resistance gradually collapsed. In February 1943, the remaining troops surrendered, marking one of the largest defeats in German military history. Hundreds of thousands had been killed, captured, or wounded. The loss of the Sixth Army was a major turning point on the Eastern Front, ending German advances into the Soviet Union and shifting momentum toward the Red Army, the official name for the Soviet Union's military forces.

54. The Desert Advance

By mid-1942, Axis forces under Erwin Rommel had pushed across North Africa from Libya into Egypt, bringing the war dangerously close to the Suez Canal. This canal was one of the most important routes in the world, linking the Mediterranean Sea to the Indian Ocean and allowing Britain to move troops and supplies quickly between Europe, Asia, and its overseas territories. If it fell, Allied communication lines would be severely disrupted. The advance finally stalled near El Alamein, a narrow stretch of desert between the Mediterranean coast and impassable terrain to the south. This geography meant that neither side could easily outflank the other, forcing a direct confrontation. Both armies dug in, building defensive lines and preparing for a decisive battle that would determine control of North Africa.

55. Breaking the Axis Line at El Alamein

In October 1942, British forces launched a carefully planned offensive at El Alamein, combining artillery barrages, infantry advances, and coordinated tank assaults to break through Axis defenses. The battle lasted nearly two weeks, with heavy fighting as minefields were cleared and fortified positions attacked. Gradually, Allied forces created gaps in the defensive lines, allowing armored units to push through. Once the line was broken, Axis forces were forced into a retreat westward across Libya, abandoning equipment as they withdrew. The victory marked the first major land defeat of German-led forces in the war and boosted Allied morale at a critical moment. It also secured Egypt and the Suez Canal, ensuring that this vital supply route remained open and allowing the Allies to begin pushing Axis forces out of North Africa entirely.

56. Landings in North Africa

In November 1942, Allied forces launched Operation Torch, a large amphibious invasion of North Africa: attacks launched from the sea onto defended coastlines. Troops from the United States and the United Kingdom landed along the coasts of Morocco and Algeria, territories controlled by the Vichy French government, which had been aligned with Germany. The goal was to open a second front in North Africa and trap Axis forces between advancing Allied armies from both east and west. After initial resistance and negotiation, many French forces ceased fighting and joined the Allies. The landings marked the first large-scale American ground operation in the European–African theater and signaled a growing Allied ability to coordinate complex operations across long distances.

57. Axis Forces in Tunisia

Following the landings of Operation Torch, Axis forces in North Africa found themselves caught between two advancing armies. From the east, British forces pushed westward after their victory at El Alamein, while American and British units moved east from newly secured positions in Algeria. The remaining Axis troops, including German and Italian units, retreated into Tunisia, where they attempted to hold defensive positions. Fighting in this region was intense, with both sides struggling over supply lines, mountainous terrain, and key ports. However, the Axis position became increasingly untenable as Allied forces tightened their grip, cutting off escape routes and reducing access to supplies. What had once been a campaign of movement across open desert turned into a confined struggle with limited options for retreat.

58. The Collapse of Axis North Africa

By May 1943, Axis resistance in North Africa had collapsed. Surrounded and cut off from reinforcement, more than 250,000 German and Italian troops surrendered in Tunisia. This marked the complete loss of Axis presence on the African continent and removed the threat to the Suez Canal. The victory gave the Allies control of the Mediterranean's southern shores and provided a launching point for further operations into southern Europe. It also demonstrated the growing strength of Allied cooperation, combining resources, troops, and planning across multiple nations. With

North Africa secured, attention shifted toward the next phase of the war: an invasion of Axis-controlled Europe.

59. Invasion of Sicily and the Opening of Italy

In July 1943, Allied forces launched Operation Husky, a massive invasion of the island of Sicily, located just off the "toe" of the Italian mainland. This was one of the largest amphibious operations of the war, involving a coordinated assault by land, sea, and air. British and American forces, led by Generals Bernard Montgomery and George S. Patton, landed on the island's southern and eastern shores to open a direct path into Southern Europe, often referred to by Winston Churchill as the "soft underbelly" of the Axis powers. Despite facing strong resistance from German and Italian divisions, the Allied forces used their superior air power and naval support to push the Axis troops across the rugged, mountainous terrain of the island. The fighting was intense, especially around the slopes of Mount Etna, but the momentum remained with the Allies. As the invasion progressed, it exposed deep-seated weaknesses within the Italian military and triggered political instability in Rome. The Italian people and many government officials were becoming weary of a war that had now reached their own soil. By August 1943, the Allies had successfully captured the island, giving them control of critical airfields and shipping routes that secured the central Mediterranean for their convoys. The capture of Sicily marked the end of the African and Mediterranean island campaigns and the beginning of the grueling struggle for the Italian mainland.

60. The Fall of Mussolini

In July 1943, the invasion of Sicily exposed deep weaknesses within Italy and shook confidence in its leadership. Benito Mussolini, who had ruled as a dictator since the 1920s, faced growing criticism from military leaders and government officials who believed the war was being lost. On July 25, 1943, he was removed from power by members of his own government and arrested on the orders of the king. A new Italian administration began secret negotiations with the Allies, seeking a way out of the conflict. Mussolini's fall marked a major political shift within the Axis alliance, showing that one of Germany's key partners was beginning to collapse under the pressure of military defeats.

61. Changing Sides in the War

In September 1943, the new Italian government signed an armistice with the Allies, effectively withdrawing from the war against them. However, the announcement created immediate confusion across the country, leaving Italian forces without clear orders as German troops moved quickly to take control. Instead of leaving Italy, Germany treated the armistice as a betrayal and launched operations to occupy the country. Italian soldiers were disarmed, captured, or forced to choose between joining German forces or resisting them. Some units fought alongside the Allies, while others were taken prisoner. The sudden shift turned Italy into a new battleground, where former allies were now fighting each other.

62. Germany's Occupation

After Italy's surrender, German forces rapidly moved to secure key cities, transportation routes, and defensive positions across the Italian peninsula. Key cities, railways, and communication routes were occupied, while Italian units were disarmed or captured. German commanders understood that Italy's geography, long, narrow, and dominated by mountains, could be used to slow any invasion. They began constructing defensive lines across the peninsula, positioning troops behind rivers, hills, and fortified positions. These defenses were designed not to win a quick victory but to delay Allied progress for as long as possible, turning Italy into a prolonged battleground that would absorb large numbers of troops and resources.

63. Mussolini Restored

At the same time, German forces carried out a dramatic rescue of Benito Mussolini, who had been imprisoned after his removal from power. In a carefully planned airborne and commando operation, he was freed and brought under German protection. Mussolini was then placed at the head of a new pro-German government in northern Italy, creating what was effectively a separate state aligned with Germany. This division split the country into two: the south, controlled by Allied forces and the new Italian government, and the north, under German occupation and Mussolini's authority. The situation led to internal conflict, as resistance groups formed to fight against German control and the new regime. Italy became not only a front line in the war but also a country divided by civil war, with fighting taking place between opposing Italian forces and foreign armies.

64. A Slow and Costly Advance

Allied forces began moving north through Italy, but the campaign proved far more difficult than expected. The terrain, mountains, rivers, and narrow valleys favored the defenders, allowing German forces to build fortified lines and delay progress. Battles were fought for control of key positions, including towns, roads, and bridges, often at high cost. Progress was slow, measured in miles rather than large advances, and each defensive line required intense fighting to break through. The campaign tied down large numbers of troops on both sides, turning Italy into a prolonged and difficult front. While it didn't bring a quick victory, it forced Germany to divert resources that might otherwise have been used elsewhere.

65. Fire from the Sky over Germany

By 1943, the Allies had begun a sustained strategic bombing campaign against Germany, aimed at weakening its capacity to wage war by targeting industry, transportation, and production centers. Strategic bombing focused on factories, railways, and fuel facilities rather than front-line troops. During the day, American bombers attempted more precise strikes, while at night, British aircraft carried out large-scale raids designed to overwhelm defenses. Cities such as Hamburg were hit with massive bombing campaigns, including incendiary bombs that started widespread fires. In some cases, these fires merged into firestorms, intense blazes that created powerful winds and consumed entire neighborhoods. The bombing caused heavy destruction and civilian casualties, but it also forced Germany to divert aircraft, anti-aircraft weapons, and manpower away from the front lines to defend its cities.

66. The Battle of Kursk Begins

In July 1943, German forces launched a major offensive against Soviet positions near Kursk (a city in western Russia), aiming to regain momentum after earlier defeats. The front line in this area formed a large bulge, making it a target for an encirclement attack from both north and south. However, Soviet commanders had anticipated the assault and built extensive defensive systems. These included multiple layers of trenches, barbed wire, anti-tank obstacles, and dense minefields designed to slow advancing units. When the German attack began, their tanks and infantry encountered fierce resistance and prepared defenses, reducing the effectiveness of their initial assault and turning what was meant to be a fast breakthrough into a prolonged battle.

67. The Largest Tank Battle

As the fighting around Kursk intensified, it developed into one of the largest armored battles ever fought. Thousands of tanks from both sides clashed across open fields and defensive positions, with close-range engagements and heavy losses. One of the most famous encounters took place near Prokhorovka on July 12, where hundreds of German and Soviet tanks collided in a chaotic, smoke-filled whirlwind of fire. The noise and dust were so thick that tank commanders often couldn't tell friend from foe until they were right on top of each other. Despite the massive scale of the attack and the introduction of powerful new German tanks, such as the *Panther* and *Tiger*, German forces failed to achieve a decisive breakthrough. The Soviet defenses, which were deeper and more sophisticated than anything the Germans had faced before, held firm. Reserves, extra troops, and equipment held back for emergencies were committed by Soviet commanders at key moments to plug gaps in the line. The failure of the Kursk offensive marked the final turning point on the Eastern Front.

68. The Red Army Pushing West

After halting the German advance at Kursk, Soviet forces launched a series of counteroffensives that pushed German troops westward. Large areas of previously occupied territory were recaptured, including important cities and industrial regions. The Red Army, strengthened by increasing production and experience, began to maintain the initiative. German forces, which had once advanced rapidly, were now forced into defensive positions, attempting to slow the Soviet advance. The scale of operations remained immense, with millions of soldiers involved and continuous fighting across a vast front. From this point onward, the momentum on the Eastern Front increasingly shifted toward the Soviet Union.

69. The Planning of D-Day

By early 1944, Allied leaders finalized plans for a massive invasion of German-occupied France, intended to open a western front against Germany and relieve pressure on the Soviet Union. The operation required unprecedented coordination between land, sea, and air forces. Thousands of ships, landing craft, and aircraft were assembled, while troops trained extensively for amphibious assaults. To increase the chances of success, the Allies also carried out an elaborate deception campaign, creating dummy armies, dummy equipment, and false radio signals to mislead German commanders into believing that the invasion would take place elsewhere, particularly near the Pas de Calais. The goal was to delay German reinforcements when the real landings began. After years of preparation, the Allies were ready to attempt one of the largest military operations in history.

70. The Landings in Normandy

On June 6, 1944, Allied forces launched the invasion of Normandy, commonly known as D-Day. Thousands of ships crossed the English Channel, carrying troops toward heavily defended beaches along the northern coast of France. The landings were divided across several sectors, each assigned to different Allied forces. Soldiers faced strong resistance as they approached the shore, with machine guns, artillery, and obstacles designed to destroy landing craft. Despite heavy casualties, especially on beaches such as Omaha, troops managed to establish footholds. Airborne units dropped behind enemy lines to disrupt defenses and secure key routes. By the end of the day, the Allies had successfully landed large numbers of troops and equipment, marking the beginning of a sustained campaign to push inland.

71. Breaking Out of Normandy

After securing the beaches in Normandy, Allied forces faced weeks of difficult fighting as they attempted to advance inland. The region's landscape, known as bocage, consisted of small fields separated by thick hedgerows, which limited visibility and favored defenders. German troops used these natural barriers to slow the advance, forcing Allied units to fight for each field and road. Progress was slow and costly, but continuous pressure, combined with air superiority and increasing reinforcements, gradually weakened German defenses. In late July 1944, Allied forces launched a breakout operation, using concentrated air bombardment to break through German lines. Once the defenses collapsed, armored units advanced rapidly, beginning the liberation of France.

72. The Liberation of Paris

As Allied forces advanced deeper into France, resistance movements in Paris began to intensify against the German occupation. In August 1944, fighting broke out in the city as resistance fighters took control of key buildings and streets. Allied troops advanced toward Paris, and German forces, facing pressure on multiple fronts, withdrew. On August 25, 1944, the city was liberated. Crowds filled the streets as Allied soldiers entered, marking a symbolic and strategic victory. The liberation of Paris not only restored a major European capital but also signaled that German control in Western Europe was beginning to collapse. The focus of the war in the west now shifted toward pushing into Germany itself.

73. A Risky Airborne Gamble

In September 1944, the Allies launched an ambitious operation called Operation Market Garden, aiming to end the war quickly by advancing into Germany through the Netherlands. The plan combined airborne troops, soldiers dropped by parachute, with ground forces moving north to link up with them. Airborne divisions were tasked with capturing a series of key bridges over rivers and canals, allowing armored units to cross quickly and bypass German defenses. If successful, the operation could have opened a direct route into Germany's industrial heartland. However, the plan depended on precise timing and underestimated German strength in the area. Some bridges were captured, but others proved heavily defended, and delays slowed the advance. The operation ultimately failed to achieve its objectives, showing that even bold strategies could falter when conditions on the ground didn't match expectations.

74. A Narrow Corridor Under Pressure

As part of Operation Market Garden, Allied ground forces advanced along a single narrow road through the Netherlands, attempting to reach airborne units holding bridges farther ahead. This route became highly vulnerable, as German forces attacked from both sides, cutting supply lines and isolating forward units. In places such as Arnhem, airborne troops held their positions for days despite being surrounded, but reinforcements failed to arrive in time. The difficulty of maintaining such a narrow corridor revealed the risks of prioritizing speed over security. When the operation ended, the Allies had gained some territory but failed to secure the final objectives, leaving the war in Western Europe far from over.

75. Germany's Last Major Offensive

In December 1944, Hitler launched a massive, surprise counteroffensive through the Ardennes Forest, the same rugged terrain he had used to invade France in 1940. His goal was to split the British and American armies, capture the vital Belgian port of Antwerp, and force the Western Allies to sign a separate peace treaty. This became known as the Battle of the Bulge because the German attack pushed a sixty-mile (or ninety-seven-kilometer) "bulge" into the Allied front lines. Taking advantage of poor weather that limited Allied air power, German troops broke through lightly defended lines and created a large bulge in the front. The sudden attack caught Allied commanders off guard, and intense fighting followed as both sides struggled for control. Towns and road junctions became key objectives, and supply shortages affected troops on both sides during the harsh winter conditions.

76. Holding the Line and Pushing Back

Despite early German success in the Battle of the Bulge, Allied forces regrouped and reinforced key positions. Small groups of American soldiers held critical crossroads, such as the town of Bastogne, where they were completely surrounded but famously refused to surrender. These pockets of resistance slowed the German advance, forcing their tanks to burn through limited fuel while waiting for roads to clear. As the weather finally cleared in late December, the Allied air forces returned to the skies with a vengeance. They targeted German supply lines, the convoys of trucks carrying the fuel and ammunition needed to keep the tanks moving. Without gasoline, many German *Tiger* and *Panther* tanks were simply abandoned in the snow. By January 1945, a massive Allied counterattack led by General Patton's Third Army pushed the front back to its original position. The failed offensive was a catastrophe for Germany; it exhausted its final reserves for the defense of the homeland. With the "bulge" flattened and the German army depleted, the path into the heart of Germany was now wide open, and the end of the war in Europe was finally in sight. As weather conditions improved, Allied air forces returned, targeting German supply lines and movements. Gradually, the German offensive lost momentum, and counterattacks pushed the front back to its previous positions by January 1945. The failed offensive exhausted Germany's remaining reserves of troops, fuel, and equipment. It was the last major attempt by Germany to regain the initiative in the west, and after its failure, the path into Germany itself became increasingly open to Allied forces.

77. The Soviet Advance

By early 1945, the Soviet Union had built up massive forces along the eastern front and launched a large-scale offensive into German-held territory. Beginning in January, Soviet armies pushed westward from Poland toward Germany, advancing rapidly across frozen ground that allowed tanks and vehicles to move more easily. German defenses, weakened by earlier losses, struggled to hold the line. Entire regions were overrun as Soviet troops captured cities, railways, and supply centers. The speed of the advance surprised many observers, as Soviet forces covered vast distances in a short time. Civilians fled westward ahead of the front, while German units attempted to regroup and delay the advance. The offensive brought Soviet forces to the borders of Germany itself, marking the beginning of the final assault on the country.

78. Crossing into Germany

At the same time, Allied forces in the west prepared to cross into Germany. One of the key obstacles was the Rhine River, a major natural barrier that German forces used as a defensive line. In March 1945, Allied troops managed to capture a bridge over the river intact, allowing them to move forces across more quickly than expected. Additional crossings followed, supported by large numbers of engineers building temporary bridges under difficult conditions. Once across the Rhine, Allied armies advanced deeper into Germany, capturing industrial regions and surrounding enemy forces. The coordinated pressure from both east and west placed Germany in an increasingly difficult position, as it faced advancing armies on multiple fronts with limited resources remaining.

79. The Encirclement of Berlin

By April 1945, the Red Army had positioned over 2.5 million troops and 6,000 tanks on the outskirts of the German capital. On April 16, they launched their final massive assault, beginning with a thunderous barrage from thousands of heavy artillery, large-caliber guns, and rocket launchers, such as the famous *Katyusha*, designed to destroy fortifications from a distance. Multiple Soviet armies, led by Marshals Zhukov and Konev, raced to be the first to reach the city center. By April 25, Berlin was completely surrounded, cutting off all escape. The defending German forces were a desperate mix of exhausted regular soldiers and the Volkssturm, a national militia consisting of "volunteers" as young as sixteen and as old as sixty, most of whom had little combat experience and were armed with basic anti-tank weapons like the *Panzerfaust*. Fighting took place street by street as Soviet forces pushed into the city. Artillery bombardments and air attacks caused widespread destruction, reducing large areas to rubble. The encirclement meant that German forces inside the city were isolated, with little chance of reinforcement or supply. The battle for Berlin became the final major confrontation in Europe, signaling that the war was nearing its end.

80. The Final Battle

By April 1945, Soviet forces had surrounded Berlin, launching a full-scale assault on the German capital. The climax of the battle took place at the Reichstag, the German parliament building, which became a symbol of the

Nazi regime. Soviet soldiers fought through the smoke-filled halls in a brutal struggle for every floor. Supply lines had collapsed, and communication between units became increasingly difficult. Civilians remained trapped in the city as the battle intensified, sheltering underground while bombardments continued. The fighting was among the most intense of the war, marking the final major confrontation in Europe.

81. Hitler's Death and the Collapse of Leadership

As Soviet troops closed in on Berlin, the leadership of Nazi Germany faced complete collapse. On April 30, 1945, as Soviet troops were just blocks away from his underground bunker, Adolf Hitler committed suicide. The government's command passed to the remaining officials, but the situation was beyond recovery. German forces in Berlin, cut off from reinforcements and supplies, could no longer sustain organized resistance. Within days, the city fell to Soviet troops, and the central government effectively ceased to function. With its capital captured and leadership gone, Germany's ability to continue the war was destroyed. The fall of Berlin made surrender inevitable, as Allied forces advanced across the remaining territory and German command structures disintegrated.

82. Germany's Unconditional Surrender

After the fall of Berlin and the collapse of central leadership, Germany's remaining officials sought to end the fighting. On May 7–8, 1945, representatives of the German military signed documents of unconditional surrender, agreeing to cease all hostilities. The surrender meant that German forces across Europe were ordered to lay down their arms. The date became known as Victory in Europe Day, or V-E Day, marking the end of the war on the European continent. However, the exact end of the conflict remained a subject of debate in some contexts, as formal arrangements and occupation agreements continued afterward. Despite these complexities, May 1945 is widely recognized as the moment when Nazi Germany was defeated, and the European war came to a close.

83. The Pacific War Continues

Although fighting had ended in Europe, the war in the Pacific continued. Japan still controlled territory across parts of Asia and the Pacific, and Allied forces prepared for a final push toward the Japanese home islands. The fighting in this region was intense, with battles taking place on islands where defenders often fought to the end rather than surrender. Allied strategy focused on capturing key islands that could serve as bases for air attacks and supply routes. At the same time, naval forces enforced blockades that limited Japan's access to resources. The conflict in the Pacific had already been long and costly, and planners expected that an invasion of Japan itself would result in even greater casualties on both sides.

84. Firebombing and the Destruction of Cities

By 1945, Allied forces intensified bombing campaigns against Japanese cities in an effort to weaken industrial production and reduce morale. Using large numbers of aircraft, they dropped incendiary bombs designed to start fires in densely built urban areas. One of the most devastating raids took place in Tokyo in March 1945, where fires spread rapidly through wooden buildings, destroying large sections of the city. These attacks caused massive destruction and high civilian casualties. At the same time, Japan's ability to respond was weakened by fuel shortages and the loss of experienced pilots. The bombing campaigns demonstrated the increasing scale of destruction in modern warfare, where entire cities could be targeted as part of military strategy.

85. The Bombing of Hiroshima

On August 6, 1945, the United States dropped an atomic bomb on the Japanese city of Hiroshima. The weapon released energy from a nuclear reaction, producing an explosion far more powerful than conventional bombs. A blinding flash was followed by an intense blast wave and extreme heat that destroyed buildings across a wide area. Many people were killed instantly, while others suffered severe burns and injuries. The explosion also released radiation, energy that can damage human tissue, which caused long-term illness and death among survivors. It is estimated that approximately 70,000–80,000 people were killed immediately, with the total death toll rising to around 140,000 by the end of 1945 due to injuries and radiation exposure. Because Hiroshima was a military and industrial center, it had been selected as a target, but the scale of destruction shocked observers. The bombing demonstrated a new level of destructive capability, where a single weapon could devastate an entire city in moments.

86. Nagasaki and the Impact of Nuclear Warfare

Three days later, on August 9, 1945, a second atomic bomb was dropped on the city of Nagasaki. Although the terrain of the city limited some of the blast's spread, the explosion still caused widespread destruction and heavy casualties. It is estimated that approximately 40,000 people were killed instantly, with the total number of deaths rising to around 70,000 by the end of 1945 as a result of injuries and radiation exposure. The use of two atomic bombs within days highlighted the destructive potential of nuclear weapons and signaled that further attacks could follow. At the same time, the Soviet Union declared war on Japan and launched a large-scale invasion of Japanese-held territory in Manchuria, adding additional pressure. Faced with the combined impact of atomic bombings and military advances, Japanese leaders began to consider surrender. The events marked the beginning of a new era in warfare, where the threat of nuclear weapons would shape global politics for decades to come.

87. The Decision to Surrender

After the atomic bombings of Hiroshima and Nagasaki and the entry of the Soviet Union into the war against Japan in August 1945, Japanese leaders faced a situation with few remaining options. Continued resistance risked further destruction, while surrender raised concerns about political and national consequences. Within the Japanese government, intense debate took place over whether to accept Allied terms. Ultimately, Emperor Hirohito intervened, supporting the decision to surrender in order to prevent further loss of life. This moment was unusual, as the emperor rarely took direct part in political decisions. The decision marked a turning point, as it set in motion the formal end of World War II, though the process would unfold over several days.

88. The Emperor's Broadcast

On August 15, 1945, Emperor Hirohito addressed the Japanese people in a radio broadcast, announcing the decision to accept Allied terms. This was the first time many citizens had ever heard the emperor's voice. The speech used formal and indirect language, referring to the need to "endure the unendurable" to achieve peace. For many listeners, the meaning wasn't immediately clear, but it soon became understood that Japan had agreed to surrender. The date became known as Victory over Japan Day, or V-J Day, and is often considered the practical end of the war, as fighting largely ceased following the announcement. However, the formal conclusion of the conflict had not yet taken place.

89. The Formal Surrender Ceremony

Although Japan announced its surrender in August, the official signing took place on September 2, 1945, aboard the American battleship USS *Missouri* in Tokyo Bay. Representatives of Japan signed documents accepting unconditional surrender in the presence of Allied officials. This ceremony formally ended the war in Asia and is often considered the definitive end of World War II. However, the exact end date of the conflict is sometimes debated, as different events marked different stages of its conclusion. While August 15 marked the announcement of surrender, September 2 marked its formal completion.

90. When Did World War II Really End?

Although World War II is commonly said to have ended in 1945, historians sometimes cite different dates depending on the context. The armistice on August 15, 1945, marked the end of active fighting, while the formal surrender on September 2 finalized the conflict. A peace treaty between Japan and the Allies was signed in 1951, officially restoring diplomatic relations. In Europe, Germany's defeat in May 1945 ended fighting there, but formal arrangements and political changes continued for years afterward. Some scholars even note that no formal peace treaty was ever signed between Japan and the Soviet Union, with relations normalized later through agreements rather than a full treaty. These variations show that the "end" of the war wasn't a single moment but a process that unfolded over time.

TWO

Dictators, Democracies, and Decisions

World War II was not only a clash of armies but also a struggle shaped by political systems, leadership, and critical decisions made under pressure. The rise of authoritarian regimes in Germany, Italy, and Japan challenged the existing international order, while democratic nations were forced to respond to growing aggression and instability. Choices made by leaders, whether to resist, negotiate, or expand, played a decisive role in determining the course of the war. This chapter examines the political forces behind the conflict, including the ambitions of dictators, the responses of democratic governments, and the key decisions that escalated tensions into full-scale war. It looks at how ideology, diplomacy, and miscalculation combined to shape events, often with far-reaching consequences.

91. A Fragile Peace and Unstable Democracies

After World War I ended in 1918, many hoped that the world had entered a more peaceful era. Instead, the postwar settlement created new tensions that weakened many governments. The Treaty of Versailles imposed heavy penalties on Germany, including financial reparations, territorial losses, and military restrictions. While intended to prevent future conflict, these measures instead fueled resentment and economic instability. At the same time, new nations emerged in Eastern Europe, but many were politically fragile and divided along ethnic lines. Democratic governments struggled to maintain authority in this environment. Many countries faced high inflation, unemployment, and political violence. In Germany, for example, the Weimar Republic, a democratic government, was attacked by both communist and nationalist groups. Communism is a political and economic system in which the government or community owns all property and resources, aiming to create a society without social classes. Across Europe, faith in democracy began to weaken as people lost trust in leaders who seemed unable to solve economic crises. This instability created conditions in which more extreme political movements could gain support by promising order, strength, and national revival.

92. Lenin's New Economic Policy and Strategic Retreat

In the early 1920s, the newly formed Soviet Union faced serious economic and social problems after years of revolution and civil war. Agricultural production had collapsed, cities were struggling with food shortages, and widespread unrest threatened the survival of the Bolshevik government. In response, Vladimir Lenin introduced the New Economic Policy (NEP) in 1921, a temporary shift away from strict communist control. The NEP allowed limited private business activity, especially in agriculture and small industries, while the state retained control over major sectors, such as heavy industry and banking. This mixed system helped stabilize the economy, increase food production, and reduce public unrest. However, it also showed that even revolutionary leaders sometimes had to compromise their ideological goals to maintain power. The policy strengthened the Soviet state in the short term, but it also raised questions about the future direction of the country, setting the stage for later struggles over how the Soviet Union should develop under new leadership.

93. The March on Rome and the Seizure of Power

In October 1922, Italy became one of the first countries in Europe to turn toward authoritarian rule when Benito Mussolini and his fascist movement took control. Italy had emerged from World War I on the winning side, but many citizens felt "cheated" by the peace settlement, believing their country had not gained enough territory or respect. Economic problems, high unemployment, and political unrest created an atmosphere of instability. During this time, Italy was a battleground between two opposing ideologies: socialism, a theory arguing that the community should own or control the means of production to ensure that wealth is distributed equally, and fascism, a far-right system that places the nation above the individual and uses a dictator to suppress opposition through force. Mussolini, a former socialist who had turned into a radical nationalist, organized his supporters into paramilitary groups known as the "Blackshirts." These groups used violence and intimidation against political opponents, especially socialists and trade unions, which are organized groups of workers formed to protect their rights and interests. In October 1922, thousands of fascist supporters began the March on Rome. While the march was largely a show of force rather than a military invasion, it created so much pressure that King Victor Emmanuel III feared a civil war. Instead of using the army to stop them, he invited Mussolini to form a government. This decision marked the beginning of a fascist dictatorship that would last for more than two decades, providing a blueprint for other future dictators, including Adolf Hitler.

94. Fascism as a Model of Authoritarian Rule

After gaining power, Mussolini gradually transformed Italy from a constitutional monarchy into a one-party dictatorship. Elections were manipulated, opposition parties were banned, and the press was placed under strict control. The state promoted a powerful nationalist message, emphasizing unity, strength, and loyalty to the leader, who was known as *Il Duce*. Political dissent was suppressed through secret police and imprisonment, creating an atmosphere of fear that limited resistance. Fascism presented itself as an alternative to both liberal democracy and communism. It rejected the idea of individual political freedoms in favor of a strong, centralized state that would guide the nation toward greatness. Mussolini's regime also promoted militarism and expansion, arguing that Italy needed to become a major power. His success in consolidating control attracted attention in other countries, particularly in Germany, where similar ideas were gaining support. Fascist Italy became an early example of how democratic systems could collapse under pressure, providing a model that would influence other authoritarian movements in the years leading up to World War II.

95. The Beer Hall Putsch and a Failed Coup

In November 1923, Adolf Hitler attempted to seize power in Germany through a coup known as the Beer Hall Putsch. At the time, Germany was facing a severe economic crisis, including hyperinflation that made money nearly worthless and widespread political instability. Hitler, who led the National Socialist German Workers' Party (Nazi Party), believed the government was weak and could be overthrown by force. On November 8, Hitler and around 2,000 supporters stormed a large political meeting in Munich, hoping to gain support from local leaders and then march on

Berlin to take control of the country. The following day, the group marched through the streets, but they were met by police forces. A brief exchange of gunfire ended the attempted coup, leaving several people dead, and the march quickly collapsed. Hitler was arrested soon afterward and charged with treason. Although the putsch failed, it revealed Hitler's ambitions and brought him national attention. Instead of ending his political career, the event would ultimately help transform him into a prominent figure in German politics.

96. Prison, Propaganda, and Political Strategy

After the failed coup, Adolf Hitler was put on trial in early 1924. Rather than weakening him, the trial became a platform for his ideas. He used the courtroom to criticize the German government and promote his nationalist and anti-Semitic beliefs (the prejudice, discrimination, or hatred directed specifically toward Jewish people), gaining sympathy from some sections of the public who saw him as a patriot rather than a criminal. He was found guilty of treason but received a relatively lenient sentence of five years in prison, of which he served only about nine months. During his imprisonment, Hitler wrote *Mein Kampf* ("My Struggle"), a book outlining his ideology and long-term goals. It included his belief in racial hierarchy, his desire to expand German territory in Eastern Europe, and his deep hostility toward Jews and communism. Importantly, the failure of the Beer Hall Putsch led him to change tactics. Instead of trying to seize power by force, he decided that the Nazi Party would pursue control through legal political means, using elections, propaganda, and influence within existing institutions. This strategic shift would later prove far more effective.

97. Stalin's Reign

In Russia, when Vladimir Lenin suffered a series of strokes beginning in 1922 and died in January 1924, a fierce power struggle began among the leading Bolsheviks: the radical wing of the Russian Social Democratic Labor Party that had successfully seized power during the 1917 Russian Revolution. These "Bolsheviks" (meaning "those of the majority") were committed to establishing a communist state and overthrowing the old imperial system of the Tsars. Joseph Stalin, who held the seemingly administrative position of General Secretary of the Communist Party, used his control over party appointments to build a massive network of loyal supporters. While other leaders focused on public speeches and theory, Stalin focused on the "paperwork" of the party, placing his allies in key positions across the vast country and gradually removing rivals such as

Leon Trotsky, the brilliant but less politically maneuverable commander of the Red Army. By the late 1920s, Stalin had effectively secured control over the Soviet government. He turned what had originally been a collective leadership of top Bolshevik officials into a centralized system centered entirely around his own absolute authority. This shift marked the beginning of a period of total state control over every aspect of Soviet life, from the economy to personal expression, as Stalin prepared to modernize the Soviet Union at any cost.

98. The Five-Year Plans and Forced Industrialization

In 1928, Joseph Stalin launched the first of several Five-Year Plans, aiming to rapidly transform the Soviet Union from a largely agricultural society into an industrial power. The plans focused on heavy industry, including the production of steel, coal, and machinery, as the government believed that industrial strength was essential to both economic independence and military security. Massive factories were built, and millions of people moved from rural areas into cities to work in new industries. At the same time, agriculture was reorganized through a process called collectivization, in which small farms were merged into large, state-controlled units. Many peasants resisted the loss of their land and livestock, resulting in widespread repression. The state responded with force, seizing grain and punishing those who opposed the system. This contributed to severe food shortages and famines, particularly in the early 1930s. While industrial output increased significantly, the human cost was immense, and the policies strengthened the government's control over both the economy and the population.

99. Purges, Fear, and Absolute Control

By the mid-1930s, Joseph Stalin had consolidated power in the Soviet Union to such an extent that he began eliminating real and perceived rivals in a series of campaigns known as the Great Purges. Between 1936 and 1938, party officials, military leaders, intellectuals, and ordinary citizens were arrested, imprisoned, or executed. Many were accused of vague crimes such as "counter-revolutionary activity" or disloyalty to the state, often based on forced confessions obtained under torture. Public trials were staged to demonstrate the consequences of opposing the regime, while the secret police, known as the NKVD, carried out mass arrests across the country. Millions of people were sent to labor camps, where harsh conditions led to high mortality rates. Even senior officers in the Red Army were removed, weakening the military's leadership on the eve of war. The purges created a climate of fear in which few dared to speak openly, allowing Stalin to maintain near-total control over the Soviet state while ensuring that any opposition was quickly and decisively crushed.

100. Political Violence and Militarism in Japan

During the early 1930s, Japan experienced growing political instability as military leaders gained increasing influence over the government. Many officers believed that Japan needed to expand its territory to secure natural resources and protect itself from foreign powers. Civilian politicians who supported diplomacy and international agreements were often seen as weak, and some became targets of violent opposition. In May 1932, a group of naval officers assassinated Prime Minister Inukai Tsuyoshi, an event known as the May 15 Incident. The attackers hoped to replace civilian leadership with a more aggressive, nationalist government. Although the coup itself didn't fully succeed, the response was relatively lenient, and public sympathy for the perpetrators weakened respect for democratic institutions. Over time, the military gained greater control over national policy, shaping decisions on foreign expansion and war. By the mid-1930s, Japan was increasingly governed by leaders who favored military solutions, setting the stage for further conflict in Asia and the Pacific.

101. Economic Crisis and the Collapse of Democracy

The global economic crisis that began in 1929, known as the Great Depression, had a devastating impact on many countries, but it was especially severe in Germany. The economy depended heavily on foreign loans, particularly from the United States, and when those loans were withdrawn, businesses collapsed, banks failed, and unemployment rose dramatically. By the early 1930s, millions of Germans were unemployed, and many families struggled to afford basic necessities. This economic hardship weakened faith in democratic government. The Weimar Republic, Germany's post–World War I government, appeared unable to solve the crisis, and political parties became increasingly divided. Extremist movements on both the left and right gained support by promising strong leadership and quick solutions. Street violence between rival groups became common, and elections produced unstable coalitions that couldn't govern effectively. As confidence in democratic institutions declined, more people began to support parties that offered radical change, creating the conditions that allowed authoritarian leaders to rise to power through legal means.

102. Hitler's Legal Path to Dictatorship

In January 1933, Adolf Hitler was appointed Chancellor of Germany after his Nazi Party became the largest political force in the country. Although he had not won an outright majority, conservative leaders believed they could control him and use his popularity to stabilize the government. This decision would prove to be a critical miscalculation. Soon after taking office, Hitler moved quickly to expand his power. In February 1933, the Reichstag building, home of the German parliament, was set on fire. The government blamed communist groups and used the crisis to suspend civil liberties, allowing the arrest of political opponents. In March, the Enabling Act was passed, giving Hitler the authority to make laws without parliamentary approval. This effectively ended democratic rule in Germany. Political parties were banned, trade unions were dissolved, and opposition leaders were imprisoned. Within months, Germany had been transformed from a democracy into a one-party dictatorship, with power concentrated entirely in Hitler's hands.

103. Rearmament and the Breaking of Versailles

After consolidating power, Adolf Hitler began to openly challenge the Treaty of Versailles, the agreement that had ended World War I and imposed strict limits on Germany's military. The treaty restricted the size of the German army, banned tanks and aircraft, and prohibited the remilitarization of certain regions. Hitler rejected these restrictions, arguing that Germany needed to restore its strength and dignity. In 1935, Germany reintroduced conscription, requiring men to serve in the military, and began expanding its armed forces far beyond the treaty's limits. The government also invested heavily in new weapons, including modern aircraft and armored vehicles.

104. Propaganda, Control, and the Nazi State

At the same time as Germany was rearming, the Nazi regime worked to control public opinion and shape society. Propaganda played a central role in maintaining support for the government. Under the direction of Joseph Goebbels, the Ministry of Propaganda controlled newspapers, radio broadcasts, films, and cultural events. Messages were carefully designed to promote loyalty to the state, glorify Hitler as a strong leader, and present Germany as a nation rising from humiliation to power. The regime also targeted groups it considered enemies, especially Jewish people, who were blamed for Germany's problems. Laws passed in the mid-1930s, such as the

Nuremberg Laws, stripped Jewish citizens of their rights and excluded them from many areas of public life. Education, youth organizations, and public ceremonies were used to spread Nazi ideology, particularly among younger generations. By controlling both information and daily life, the government created an environment in which dissent was dangerous, and conformity was encouraged, strengthening its hold over the population as it prepared for expansion.

105. Appeasement and the Rhineland Gamble

In March 1936, Adolf Hitler took a major risk by sending German troops into the Rhineland, a region along Germany's western border that had been designated as a demilitarized zone under the Treaty of Versailles. This area was intended to serve as a buffer between Germany and France, reducing the chances of another conflict. The German military at the time was still relatively weak, and many officers were concerned that France might respond with force. However, no military action was taken. France, facing political uncertainty at home, hesitated to act without British support, and the British government viewed Germany's move as taking place within its own territory. This response reflected a broader policy known as appeasement, in which leaders hoped that allowing limited demands might prevent a larger war. The success of this gamble strengthened Hitler's position at home and convinced him that his opponents were unlikely to intervene, encouraging more aggressive actions in the years that followed.

106. The Anschluss and Expansion Without War

In March 1938, Germany annexed Austria in an event known as the Anschluss, meaning "union." Many Austrians supported unification with Germany, but the move also involved significant pressure and the threat of military force. German troops entered Austria without resistance, and a controlled referendum was later held to legitimize the annexation, producing an overwhelming but heavily influenced result in favor of joining Germany. The annexation was another clear violation of international agreements, yet once again, there was no military response from Britain or France. The incorporation of Austria increased Germany's population, territory, and access to resources, strengthening its position in Central Europe. It also placed Germany in a stronger strategic position, surrounding Czechoslovakia and opening the way for further expansion. Like the remilitarization of the Rhineland, the Anschluss demonstrated that Germany could alter the map of Europe without facing immediate consequences, further emboldening its leadership.

107. The Munich Agreement and the Sudetenland

In 1938, Adolf Hitler turned his attention to Czechoslovakia, specifically the Sudetenland, a border region with a large ethnic German population. He claimed that these communities were being mistreated and demanded that the territory be handed over to Germany. Czechoslovakia had a strong army and defensive fortifications, but it was diplomatically isolated and depended on support from Britain and France. In September 1938, leaders from Britain, France, Germany, and Italy met in Munich to resolve the crisis. Czechoslovakia itself wasn't invited to the negotiations. The resulting agreement allowed Germany to annex the Sudetenland in exchange for Hitler's promise that he would make no further territorial demands. British Prime Minister Neville Chamberlain returned home, declaring that the agreement had secured "peace for our time." However, the decision weakened Czechoslovakia by stripping away its defenses and industrial regions, while convincing Hitler that the Western powers would continue to avoid confrontation.

108. The End of Appeasement and the Road to War

The Munich Agreement didn't bring lasting peace. In March 1939, Germany violated its promises by occupying the rest of Czechoslovakia, demonstrating that Hitler's ambitions extended far beyond uniting German-speaking populations. This action shocked many in Britain and France, as it made clear that appeasement had failed to prevent further aggression. In response, both countries began to change their policies. They guaranteed the independence of Poland, warning that any attack on the country would lead to war. At the same time, Germany increased its military preparations and began making demands regarding the Polish city of Danzig and the surrounding territory. Diplomatic tensions rose rapidly across Europe as alliances hardened and negotiations broke down. By mid-1939, the situation had become increasingly unstable, with many leaders recognizing that another major conflict was becoming unavoidable. The system that had seemed fragile for years was now close to collapse.

109. Hitler's Pact with the Soviet Union

Adolf Hitler's decision to sign an agreement with the Soviet Union in August 1939 wasn't based on trust, but on strategy. Germany's leaders remembered the outcome of World War I, when fighting on two fronts, against France and Britain in the west and Russia in the east, had stretched resources and contributed to defeat. Hitler was determined to avoid repeating that mistake. At the same time, negotiations between the Soviet Union, Britain, and France had stalled. Joseph Stalin was concerned that the Western powers might be trying to push Germany and the Soviet Union into conflict while staying out of the fighting themselves. By reaching an agreement with Germany instead, Stalin gained time to rebuild his military after the purges of the late 1930s, which had removed many experienced officers. For Hitler, the pact ensured that when Germany invaded Poland, it would not immediately face Soviet resistance. For Stalin, it created a buffer zone between the Soviet Union and Germany. Both leaders viewed the agreement as temporary, expecting that conflict between them would eventually arise.

110. Calculations, Misjudgments, and the Road to War

The final days before the invasion of Poland were shaped by a series of calculated decisions and dangerous assumptions. Hitler believed that Britain and France, despite their warnings, would avoid another large-scale war, as they had done during earlier crises such as the Rhineland and Czechoslovakia. Previous success without consequences had reinforced his confidence that opponents would continue to back down. At the same time, British and French leaders believed that firm guarantees to Poland might deter Germany, or at least limit the scale of conflict. However, they lacked the immediate capacity to provide direct military support to Poland if war broke out. This created a situation in which commitments were made, but practical responses were uncertain. When Germany invaded Poland on September 1, 1939, these miscalculations became clear. Britain and France declared war two days later, but Poland faced the initial assault largely alone. What followed wasn't the limited conflict some leaders had hoped for, but the beginning of a global war shaped by earlier decisions, hesitations, and misunderstandings.

111. Different Leadership Styles

When the war began in 1939, the major powers were led by figures with very different styles of leadership, which shaped how each country fought. In Germany, Adolf Hitler increasingly took direct control of military decisions, often relying on his own judgment rather than professional advice. His leadership was centralized, personal, and driven by ideology, with little tolerance for disagreement. In contrast, Britain and France were led by civilian governments that had to balance military needs with political opinion. Decisions were slower and often cautious, especially in the early stages of the war. In the Soviet Union, Joseph Stalin ruled through a highly centralized system, but his earlier purges had removed many experienced military officers, weakening the Red Army's leadership. In Japan, decision-making was divided between civilian leaders and powerful military factions, often leading to competing strategies. These differences meant that the war wasn't only a clash of armies but also a clash of leadership styles, each with its own strengths and weaknesses.

112. The "Phoney War" and Strategic Hesitation

After Britain and France declared war on Germany in September 1939, many expected immediate large-scale fighting in Western Europe. Instead, a period of relative quiet followed, often called the "Phoney War." For several months, there was little direct combat between German forces and the Western Allies along the French-German border. French strategy relied heavily on defense, particularly the Maginot Line, a system of fortifications designed to prevent a German invasion. Military planners believed that a strong defensive position would wear down any attack. At the same time, British forces were still mobilizing and building up strength. Leaders in both countries hoped that economic pressure, such as a naval blockade, might weaken Germany over time without the need for immediate large-scale offensives. This hesitation allowed Germany to consolidate its gains in Poland and prepare for future campaigns. The lack of early action also revealed a gap between expectations and reality, as leaders struggled to adapt to a new, fast-moving, industrialized form of warfare.

113. Hitler's Risky Strategy in the West

After the defeat of Poland in 1939, German leadership turned its attention to Western Europe, where France and Britain remained at war with Germany. Many military planners initially expected a repeat of World War I, with a major attack through Belgium followed by slow, grinding battles along fortified lines. Early German plans reflected this idea, proposing a direct advance that could have led to another stalemate. However, a different approach began to take shape. German General Erich von Manstein proposed a bold alternative: instead of attacking where the Allies expected, German forces would move through the Ardennes, a heavily forested region between Belgium and France. This area was considered difficult terrain for tanks and large armies and, therefore, lightly defended. Hitler approved the plan, despite its risks, because it offered the possibility of a rapid and decisive victory. The strategy depended on speed, coordination, and surprise. If it failed, German forces could become trapped. But if it succeeded, it could break through Allied defenses and avoid the kind of prolonged war that Germany wanted to prevent.

114. The Ardennes Gamble and Allied Misjudgment

When Germany launched its offensive in May 1940, Allied leaders believed the main attack would come through northern Belgium, as it had in World War I. As a result, British and French forces moved north to meet the expected advance, leaving the Ardennes region relatively weakly defended. Many commanders considered the area unsuitable for large-scale armored movement, assuming that dense forests and narrow roads would slow any attack. This assumption proved to be a critical mistake. German armored divisions moved quickly through the Ardennes, crossing difficult terrain faster than expected and concentrating their forces at key points. Once they reached the Meuse River, German units broke through French defenses and advanced rapidly toward the English Channel. This maneuver split the Allied forces, trapping large numbers of British and French troops in northern France and Belgium. The speed of the advance shocked Allied commanders, who struggled to respond to a form of warfare that emphasized mobility and coordination rather than static defense. The success of the Ardennes plan demonstrated how assumptions based on past wars could lead to dangerous miscalculations in a new kind of conflict.

115. Command Breakdown and the Collapse of France

As German forces broke through the Ardennes in May 1940 and advanced rapidly toward the English Channel, Allied command structures struggled to respond. French and British leaders had expected a slower, more predictable campaign, and their communication systems weren't prepared for the speed of German advances. Orders were often delayed, misunderstood, or based on outdated information, making it difficult to coordinate an effective defense. French command relied on centralized decision-making, meaning that field commanders often had to wait for instructions rather than act independently. This slowed reactions at critical moments. Meanwhile, German forces operated with more flexible command structures, allowing local commanders to exploit opportunities quickly. The rapid advance cut off Allied armies in the north, while German units continued pushing deeper into France. The collapse wasn't only military but also organizational, as confusion and a lack of coordination made it increasingly difficult to mount a unified response against a fast-moving, adaptive opponent.

116. Leadership Decisions and the Fall of France

As the situation worsened, French political leaders faced a difficult choice: continue fighting or seek an armistice. By June 1940, German forces had captured Paris, and much of northern France was under occupation. The government was divided. Some leaders, including Prime Minister Paul Reynaud, wanted to continue the fight from overseas colonies, while others believed further resistance would only lead to greater destruction. Reynaud eventually resigned, and Marshal Philippe Pétain, a respected World War I general, took power. Pétain argued that continuing the war would cause unnecessary suffering and chose to request an armistice with Germany. The agreement, signed in June 1940, divided France into occupied and unoccupied zones, with a new government established in the town of Vichy. While officially neutral, this regime cooperated with Germany in many areas. The decision to surrender reshaped the balance of the war. Britain was left to face Germany largely alone in Western Europe, while France's defeat gave Germany control over significant resources and strategic positions.

117. Churchill's Leadership and the Decision to Resist

In May 1940, as German forces advanced rapidly through Western Europe, Britain faced the possibility of defeat. Neville Chamberlain resigned as prime minister, and Winston Churchill took his place at a moment of crisis. Unlike some members of the British government who considered negotiating with Germany, Churchill was determined to continue the fight, even if Britain stood alone. Churchill believed that any agreement with Hitler would only delay further conflict and weaken Britain's position. In a series of speeches, he made it clear that the country would resist invasion and continue the war regardless of the cost. His message wasn't one of easy victory but of endurance, emphasizing that survival itself was the goal. At the same time, the government began preparing for a possible invasion, strengthening defenses and organizing resources for a prolonged conflict. This decision to resist shaped the course of the war. By refusing to negotiate, Britain remained in the fight and continued to serve as a base for future Allied operations, ensuring that Germany would not achieve complete dominance in Western Europe.

118. Hitler's Strategic Choice and the Limits of Power

After the fall of France in June 1940, Adolf Hitler faced a major strategic decision. With much of Western Europe under German control, he could attempt to force Britain out of the war or turn his attention elsewhere. A full invasion of Britain, known as Operation Sea Lion, was considered, but it required control of the air and sea, which Germany didn't yet have. Instead, Germany began an air campaign aimed at weakening Britain's defenses and forcing a political settlement. Hitler still believed that Britain might eventually agree to negotiate, especially if it faced continued pressure. This assumption influenced his decision not to commit immediately to a risky cross-channel invasion. The delay allowed Britain time to strengthen its defenses and adapt to the new phase of the war. It also revealed a limitation in German strategy: success on land didn't automatically translate into control over air and sea power. Hitler's choice to postpone the invasion and rely on pressure rather than decisive action would have long-term consequences, as Britain remained in the war and continued to resist German expansion.

119. Decision-Making in the Battle of Britain

During the summer of 1940, German leadership aimed to defeat Britain by destroying its air defenses. The Luftwaffe (German air force) began a sustained campaign targeting radar stations, airfields, and aircraft production facilities in southern England. These attacks were designed to weaken the Royal Air Force (RAF) and clear the way for a possible invasion. German commanders believed that sustained pressure would eventually overwhelm British defenses. British leadership, however, relied on a coordinated system that allowed them to respond efficiently. Radar stations detected incoming aircraft, while central command centers directed fighter squadrons to intercept them at the right moment. This system helped conserve resources and avoid unnecessary losses. Fighter Command, led by Air Chief Marshal Hugh Dowding, carefully managed limited aircraft and pilots, prioritizing defense over risky offensives. The outcome of the battle depended not only on equipment but also on decision-making. British leaders focused on maintaining their defensive network, while German strategy depended on breaking it quickly. As the campaign continued, it became clear that control of the air would not be easy to achieve.

120. Strategic Shifts and the Blitz

In September 1940, German strategy changed. Instead of continuing to focus primarily on airfields and radar installations, the Luftwaffe shifted to bombing major cities, especially London. This campaign, known as the Blitz, aimed to damage infrastructure and reduce civilian morale, with the expectation that sustained bombing would pressure Britain into seeking peace. The shift, however, had unintended consequences. By reducing attacks on airfields and radar stations, German forces allowed the RAF time to recover and rebuild. British defenses remained operational, and aircraft production continued despite the damage caused by bombing. Civilians adapted by using shelters, underground stations, and emergency services to cope with the attacks. The bombing caused widespread destruction and loss of life, but it didn't achieve its primary goal of forcing Britain out of the war. By October 1940, plans for a German invasion were postponed indefinitely. The decision to change targets marked a turning point, as it reduced pressure on British air defenses and allowed them to remain a significant obstacle to German expansion.

121. Mussolini's Independent War and Strategic Overreach

After Germany's rapid victories in 1939–1940, Benito Mussolini feared that Italy might be left out of the rewards of war. Although Italy had not been fully prepared for a large-scale conflict, Mussolini decided to enter the war in June 1940, believing that Germany's success would lead to a quick victory. His decision was driven more by ambition and prestige than by military readiness. Soon after, Mussolini launched a series of independent campaigns without fully coordinating with German leadership. In October 1940, Italian forces invaded Greece from Albania, expecting an easy victory. Instead, Greek forces resisted strongly and pushed the Italians back into Albanian territory. At the same time, Italian forces in North Africa advanced into Egypt but soon faced strong British counterattacks. These campaigns revealed weaknesses in planning, logistics, and equipment. Italian forces often lacked sufficient supplies and coordination, while their opponents adapted quickly. Mussolini's decision to act independently expanded the war into new regions, but it also exposed the limits of Italy's military strength and created problems that Germany would soon have to address.

122. German Intervention and the Cost of Alliance

Italy's setbacks forced Adolf Hitler to intervene in regions he had not originally planned to prioritize. In early 1941, German forces were sent to North Africa to support Italian troops, forming the Afrika Korps under General Erwin Rommel. These forces helped stabilize the situation and pushed British units back across the desert, temporarily restoring Axis momentum in the region. At the same time, Germany prepared to intervene in the Balkans after Italy's failed invasion of Greece. German leaders were concerned that instability in southeastern Europe could threaten vital supply routes, particularly access to oil from Romania. In April 1941, German forces invaded both Yugoslavia and Greece, quickly defeating resistance and securing the region. While these interventions were successful in the short term, they came at a strategic cost. Resources and attention were diverted away from other plans, including preparations for the invasion of the Soviet Union. The need to support weaker allies showed that alliances could create new obligations, forcing leaders to adjust their strategies in ways that complicated their overall war plans.

123. Hitler's Decision to Invade the Soviet Union

In June 1941, Adolf Hitler made the decision to invade the Soviet Union, opening what would become the largest front of the war. The operation, known as Operation Barbarossa, involved millions of soldiers advancing across a vast frontier. The decision wasn't only strategic but also ideological. Hitler viewed the Soviet Union as both a political enemy and a source of land and resources that Germany needed to secure its future. German planning focused on a rapid campaign. Leaders believed that Soviet forces would collapse within a few months, allowing Germany to achieve victory before winter. The strategy relied on speed, coordination, and large-scale encirclements to destroy Soviet armies quickly. Early successes appeared to confirm these expectations, as German forces advanced deep into Soviet territory during the summer of 1941. However, the decision to launch such a massive invasion also meant committing resources to a long and uncertain campaign. By opening an eastern front while still at war with Britain, Germany entered a conflict that would strain its military and economic capacity far beyond those of earlier campaigns.

124. Underestimation and Strategic Miscalculation

German leadership underestimated both the size and resilience of the Soviet Union. Intelligence reports had suggested that the Red Army had been weakened by internal purges, and early victories reinforced the belief that resistance would collapse quickly. However, the scale of the Soviet Union's resources, territory, and population made it far more difficult to defeat than expected. As German forces advanced, supply lines became longer and more difficult to maintain. Roads were poor, distances were vast, and the infrastructure needed to support a fast-moving army was limited. At the same time, Soviet forces continued to mobilize new units, replacing losses and preparing for counterattacks. The Soviet government also relocated key industries eastward, beyond the reach of German advances, allowing production to continue. The assumption of a quick victory proved to be one of the most significant miscalculations of the war. As the conflict continued into the winter, German forces faced conditions for which they were unprepared, while Soviet resistance grew stronger. What had been planned as a short campaign became a prolonged and costly struggle that would reshape the course of the war.

125. Stalin's Shock and Sudden Recovery

When Germany invaded the Soviet Union on June 22, 1941, Joseph Stalin was reportedly caught off guard despite multiple intelligence warnings. For months, Soviet sources, including spies in Europe, had warned of a possible German attack. However, Stalin believed that Hitler would not risk a two-front war while Britain remained unconquered. He also feared that responding too aggressively to border tensions might provoke Germany prematurely. In the first days of the invasion, Stalin withdrew from public view, and confusion spread within the Soviet leadership. However, within a short period, he reasserted control. On July 3, 1941, Stalin addressed the Soviet population by radio, framing the conflict not merely as a war between governments but as a patriotic struggle for survival. This shift in messaging mobilized broader national support beyond communist ideology. The early shock revealed weaknesses in Soviet preparedness, but Stalin's decision to remain in Moscow and organize national resistance played a key role in stabilizing morale during the invasion's most dangerous phase.

126. Centralized Command and the Price of Absolute Authority

Stalin governed through strict centralization, meaning that major military decisions were often controlled from the top. While this allowed for rapid coordination of national resources, it also created serious problems during the early stages of the invasion. Soviet commanders were frequently afraid to act independently, fearing punishment if they made incorrect decisions. This hesitation sometimes slowed responses at critical moments. Earlier political purges had removed many experienced officers from the Red Army, weakening its leadership structure. As a result, the army struggled with coordination and communication during the first months of the war. Over time, however, Stalin adjusted his approach. He gradually allowed greater operational flexibility to capable commanders such as Georgy Zhukov, who would later play a major role in defending Moscow and leading counteroffensives. The Soviet system combined harsh discipline with massive mobilization. Factories were relocated east of the Ural Mountains, entire industries were reorganized, and millions of civilians were drafted into war production. While centralized authority created early setbacks, it also enabled the Soviet Union to reorganize on a vast scale, transforming initial disaster into long-term resistance.

127. Japan's Strategic Debate: North or South Expansion

During the late 1930s and early 1940s, Japanese leaders were divided over how the country should expand its influence. One group within the military supported a strategy known as "strike north," which focused on expanding into Siberia and confronting the Soviet Union. This approach aimed to secure land and resources while aligning Japan more closely with Germany's war in Europe. However, a series of border conflicts between Japanese and Soviet forces, particularly in 1939, ended in decisive Soviet victories. These defeats demonstrated the risks of confronting the Soviet Union directly and weakened support for northern expansion. At the same time, Japan faced increasing pressure from Western powers, especially the United States, which opposed its actions in China and Southeast Asia. As a result, attention shifted toward a "strike south" strategy, focusing on resource-rich regions such as Southeast Asia and the Pacific. These areas contained vital supplies like oil, rubber, and metals, which Japan needed to sustain its economy and military operations. This shift in strategy would soon bring Japan into direct conflict with Western powers.

128. The Oil Embargo

By 1941, tensions between Japan and the United States had reached a critical point. The United States had imposed economic sanctions, including restrictions on oil exports, in response to Japanese expansion in China and Southeast Asia. Since Japan depended heavily on imported resources, especially oil, these measures created a strategic dilemma. Leaders had to choose between reducing expansion and securing resources by force. Japanese leadership concluded that negotiation was unlikely to resolve the situation on favorable terms. Instead, they planned a preemptive strike to weaken American power in the Pacific. The goal was to destroy the U.S. Pacific Fleet, buying time for Japan to secure key territories before the United States could respond effectively. On December 7, 1941, Japanese aircraft attacked the U.S. naval base at Pearl Harbor in Hawaii. The attack caused significant damage to ships and aircraft and resulted in heavy casualties. While it achieved tactical surprise, it also led the United States to declare war. This decision transformed the conflict into a global war involving major powers across multiple continents and oceans.

129. Roosevelt's "Germany First" Strategy

After the attack on Pearl Harbor in December 1941, the United States entered the war facing two major enemies: Japan in the Pacific and Germany in Europe. This created a strategic dilemma. While public attention was focused on Japan, American and British leaders agreed that Germany posed the greater long-term threat due to its industrial strength, technological development, and control over much of Europe. As a result, President Franklin D. Roosevelt and Prime Minister Winston Churchill adopted what became known as the "Germany First" strategy. This approach prioritized defeating Germany before concentrating fully on Japan, even though the United States continued to fight in the Pacific. The reasoning was that if Germany were allowed to consolidate its power, it would later become far more difficult to defeat. This decision shaped the entire course of the war. Resources, production, and long-term planning were directed toward Europe, while the Pacific war was fought with more limited means in the early years. It demonstrated how strategic priorities were set not only by immediate threats but also by assessments of long-term danger.

130. Building and Coordinating a Global Alliance

Fighting a global war required cooperation between countries with different political systems, priorities, and military structures. The United States, Britain, and the Soviet Union formed the core of the Allied coalition, despite significant differences in ideology and leadership. Coordinating their efforts required constant communication and negotiation. A series of conferences helped establish shared goals and strategies. Leaders met to discuss military plans, resource allocation, and the overall direction of the war. One key principle that emerged was the demand for "unconditional surrender," meaning that the Axis powers would not be allowed to negotiate terms but would have to accept complete defeat. Cooperation extended beyond strategy. Industrial production, supply systems, and military operations had to be coordinated across continents. For example, the United States supplied large quantities of equipment and materials to its allies, while joint operations were planned to apply pressure on multiple fronts. Despite disagreements and tensions, the ability of Allied leaders to coordinate their efforts became a major factor in their eventual success. The war was no longer being fought by individual nations alone but by a coalition that combined resources on a global scale.

131. Increasing Control over Military Decisions

As the war progressed, Adolf Hitler increasingly took direct control over military decisions, reducing the influence of experienced generals. Early German successes had relied on flexibility and rapid adaptation, but over time, leadership became more centralized and less responsive to changing conditions on the battlefield. Hitler often issued detailed orders from headquarters, even when he lacked accurate, up-to-date information about the situation at the front. One of the most significant features of this approach was his insistence on holding ground at all costs. Retreats, even when they were strategically necessary, were often forbidden. German units were ordered to defend positions until the last possible moment, which frequently led to encirclement and the destruction of entire formations. Opportunities to withdraw and reorganize were lost, weakening the army's ability to sustain prolonged operations. At the same time, disagreements between Hitler and his generals over priorities became more common. Resources were sometimes spread across multiple objectives rather than concentrated where they were most effective. This combination of rigid command and divided focus gradually reduced Germany's ability to respond to setbacks, turning early advantages into long-term strategic problems.

132. Allied Flexibility and Coordinated Strategy

In contrast to the increasingly centralized and rigid command structure in Germany, Allied leadership developed a more flexible and cooperative approach as the war progressed. Although early coordination between Britain, the United States, and the Soviet Union was often difficult, these countries gradually established systems that allowed them to plan and operate together on a global scale. One key feature of this approach was the delegation of authority to experienced commanders in the field. Leaders such as Dwight D. Eisenhower and Georgy Zhukov were given the responsibility to make operational decisions based on local conditions, allowing armies to adapt more quickly to changing situations. At the same time, major strategic decisions were coordinated through conferences and joint planning bodies, ensuring that efforts across regions aligned with a common goal. The Allies also demonstrated a willingness to learn from setbacks. Early defeats led to changes in tactics, improvements in communication, and better integration of land, sea, and air forces. Over time, this adaptability allowed them to coordinate large-scale operations across multiple fronts, applying pressure simultaneously and gradually reducing the ability of Axis forces to respond effectively.

133. Opening a Second Front

One of the most important strategic debates among Allied leaders concerned when and where to open a second major front against Germany in Western Europe. The Soviet Union, which had been fighting large-scale battles on the Eastern Front since 1941, pushed strongly for an invasion of France to relieve pressure on its forces. Joseph Stalin argued that without a second front, the Soviet Union would continue to bear the main burden of the war. British and American leaders, however, were cautious. Early in the war, they believed they weren't yet prepared for a large-scale invasion of heavily defended territory. Instead, they chose to launch operations in North Africa and later in Italy, gradually building experience and weakening Axis forces. These decisions reflected both strategic caution and practical limitations in manpower, equipment, and coordination. By 1944, Allied leaders agreed that the time had come to open a second front in Western Europe. The decision required careful planning and coordination, as it would involve one of the largest amphibious operations in history. The timing and location of the invasion were chosen to maximize the chances of success while forcing Germany to fight on multiple fronts simultaneously.

134. Planning a Coordinated Invasion

The plan for the invasion of Western Europe, later known as Operation Overlord, required unprecedented coordination between Allied nations. Leaders had to consider not only military strength but also logistics, weather conditions, and the element of surprise. Large numbers of troops, vehicles, and supplies needed to be transported across the English Channel, while air and naval forces had to secure the area to support the landings. Deception played a crucial role in the planning process. This involved the use of false information, dummy equipment, and controlled communications designed to mislead German intelligence. At the same time, commanders prepared for the complexity of the operation itself. Multiple landing sites were selected, each with specific objectives, and forces from different countries were assigned to work together. The success of the invasion would depend on precise timing and coordination across land, sea, and air. The planning phase demonstrated how Allied leadership combined strategy, deception, and cooperation to prepare for one of the most critical operations of the war.

135. Leadership and the Decision to Launch D-Day

By early June 1944, Allied leaders had completed preparations for the invasion of Western Europe, but the final decision to launch the operation depended heavily on weather conditions. The invasion required calm seas, low tides, and enough light for airborne and naval forces to operate effectively. However, forecasts for early June were uncertain, and poor weather could delay the operation by weeks. General Dwight D. Eisenhower, the Supreme Allied Commander, was responsible for making the final decision. Postponing the invasion risked losing momentum and possibly revealing the plan to German forces, while proceeding under poor conditions increased the danger for troops landing on heavily defended beaches. After reviewing updated weather reports, Eisenhower chose to proceed with the invasion on June 6, 1944. The decision carried enormous consequences. Thousands of ships, aircraft, and soldiers were already in position, and reversing the operation would have been extremely difficult. By committing to the invasion, Allied leadership accepted the risks involved, relying on careful planning and coordination to achieve success.

136. Commanding Under Pressure

Once the invasion began, Allied commanders had to respond to rapidly changing conditions on the ground. Communication was often difficult, and units faced unexpected resistance in some areas. On several beaches along the Normandy coast in France, especially Omaha Beach, troops encountered strong defenses, including fortified positions, machine-gun fire, and obstacles designed to slow the landing forces. Commanders had to make quick decisions with limited information. In some cases, landing forces were scattered, requiring officers and soldiers to reorganize under fire. Naval and air support played a crucial role in suppressing defenses, while engineers worked to clear obstacles and open routes inland. Despite heavy casualties, Allied forces gradually secured their positions and established a foothold in France. The ability of commanders to adapt to unfolding events was essential to the success of the operation. The invasion demonstrated how leadership under pressure required not only planning but also flexibility and the capacity to make critical decisions in real time.

137. Stalin, Roosevelt, and Churchill: Coordinating Victory

As the war progressed into its later stages, cooperation among Allied leaders became increasingly important. The leaders of the United States, Britain, and the Soviet Union, Franklin D. Roosevelt, Winston Churchill, and Joseph Stalin, met at a series of conferences to coordinate strategy and plan for the final defeat of Germany. Despite their shared goal, the three leaders had different priorities shaped by their countries' positions and experiences in the war. The Soviet Union, having suffered enormous losses, pushed for continued pressure on Germany and the opening of additional fronts to reduce the burden on its forces. Britain and the United States focused on coordinating large-scale operations in Western Europe while maintaining supply lines and global commitments. These meetings also addressed the future of Europe, including the occupation of Germany and the political structure of liberated territories. Although disagreements were common, the ability of these leaders to maintain cooperation was crucial. Their decisions ensured that Germany faced sustained pressure from multiple directions, accelerating the collapse of its military position.

138. Political Decisions and the Shape of the War's End

As Allied forces advanced into German territory in 1944 and 1945, leaders began making decisions about how the war would end and what would follow. Leaders discussed how Germany would be governed after defeat. Plans were made to divide the country into occupation zones, each controlled by one of the major Allied powers. Similar discussions took place regarding Eastern Europe, where the Soviet Union had already established a strong military presence. These decisions weren't purely military; they were also political, shaping the postwar world. As the war drew to a close, cooperation between the Allies began to show signs of strain, as differences in ideology and interests became more pronounced. Even before the fighting had fully ended, the foundations of future tensions were already being laid.

139. Final Decisions in Berlin and the Collapse of Leadership

By April 1945, as Soviet forces closed in on Berlin, Adolf Hitler faced a situation he had long claimed would never happen: total defeat. For years, he had framed the war as a struggle in which victory or destruction were the only possible outcomes. He rejected the idea of surrender entirely, believing that if Germany couldn't win, it didn't deserve to survive. This belief shaped his final decisions. Hitler also feared capture by Soviet forces, whose advance into Germany had been accompanied by intense fighting and widespread destruction. He was determined not to be taken prisoner or publicly displayed as a defeated leader. In his final days, he dictated political statements blaming others for Germany's failures and insisting that the war had been lost due to betrayal rather than strategic mistakes. On

April 30, 1945, as Soviet troops fought nearby, Hitler ended his life in his underground bunker. His death was both a personal decision and a reflection of his refusal to accept defeat or negotiate. Even in the final moments, leadership remained tied to ideology rather than reality, leaving no organized transition or clear direction as Germany collapsed around him.

140. Leadership Decisions and the End of the War in Asia

By the summer of 1945, the United States faced a difficult decision about how to end the war with Japan. Although Japan had lost much of its navy and air power, its leadership showed no clear willingness to surrender. Previous battles, such as those on Pacific islands, had demonstrated that Japanese forces often fought to the end, raising concerns that an invasion of the Japanese mainland could result in extremely high casualties on both sides. The final decision rested with U.S. President Harry S. Truman, who had taken office in April 1945 after the death of Franklin D. Roosevelt. Truman was informed about a secret program known as the Manhattan Project, which had developed atomic weapons capable of causing unprecedented destruction. Military planners presented the bomb as a way to force a rapid surrender without the need for a full-scale invasion. On August 6 and August 9, 1945, atomic bombs were dropped on Hiroshima and Nagasaki. At the same time, the Soviet Union entered the war against Japan, launching a major offensive in Manchuria. Together, these events placed enormous pressure on Japanese leadership. Within days, Emperor Hirohito intervened to support surrender, marking a rare direct political role. The decision to use atomic weapons remains one of the most debated choices in modern history, as leaders weighed the goal of ending the war quickly against the devastating human consequences.

THREE

Intelligence & Hidden War

Behind the visible battles of World War II existed another conflict: one fought in secret. Intelligence gathering, codebreaking, and covert operations played a crucial role in shaping the outcome of campaigns, often determining success or failure long before troops engaged on the battlefield. Information became one of the most valuable weapons of the war. This chapter explores the hidden side of the conflict, from the breaking of encrypted messages to the development of advanced surveillance and deception strategies. It highlights the importance of intelligence networks and the individuals who worked behind the scenes, often without recognition, to gain an advantage over the enemy. It was a war where knowledge could be as powerful as firepower and where secrets could decide the fate of nations.

141. Early Codebreaking and the Polish Enigma Breakthrough

Before the war officially began, one of the most important intelligence battles was already underway: the effort to read German encrypted communications. Germany used a machine called Enigma, which looked like a heavy typewriter but functioned as a complex scrambling device. It was used to turn ordinary military orders into ciphertext: a jumble of letters that looked like nonsense to anyone who didn't have the correct "key" to unlock it. To a layperson, the Enigma was a mechanical puzzle of incredible complexity. Each time an operator pressed a key, three or more internal rotors (spinning wheels) would turn, constantly changing the electrical pathway and producing a different letter. Because the machine's settings were changed every single day, there were over 150 quintillion (150 followed by eighteen zeros) possible combinations. The Germans were so confident in this complexity that they believed the code was absolutely unbreakable. In the early 1930s, however, Polish mathematicians made a crucial breakthrough. Instead of using traditional linguistics (looking for patterns in language), they used mathematical analysis to figure out the internal wiring of the machine. By 1932, a mathematician named Marian Rejewski successfully reconstructed the Enigma's logic. The Poles even developed devices called "bombes," early mechanical computers designed to automate the process of guessing the daily settings. As the threat of war grew, Poland realized it could no longer keep up with the increasing complexity of German updates alone. In July 1939, just weeks before the invasion of their country, Polish intelligence shared their secret "Enigma clones" and their mathematical findings with their British and French allies.

142. Bletchley Park and the Birth of Ultra Intelligence

After receiving the Polish discoveries, Britain established a secret codebreaking center at Bletchley Park, located northwest of London. There, mathematicians, linguists, engineers, and analysts worked together to break German encrypted communications. Among them were individuals from a wide range of backgrounds, including academics, crossword puzzle experts, and chess players, all selected for their ability to recognize patterns and solve complex problems. One of the key challenges was the constant change in Enigma settings. To keep up, British codebreakers used machines known as "bombes," which could rapidly test different configurations. Over time, they began to read large volumes of German messages, an intelligence source later known as Ultra. Ultra intelligence provided detailed information about German movements, supply lines, and strategic plans. However, it had to be used carefully. If Germany realized its codes had been broken, it would change its systems. As a result, intelligence from Enigma was often disguised or used indirectly to avoid revealing the secret. This balance between using information and protecting its source became a constant challenge throughout the war.

143. Early Intelligence Failures and Missed Signals

Despite advances in codebreaking, intelligence during the early stages of the war was far from perfect. Information was often incomplete, delayed, or difficult to interpret, and even accurate intelligence could be ignored if it didn't fit existing expectations. This was especially true before major German offensives, when warning signs were sometimes overlooked. Before the German invasion of the Soviet Union in June 1941, multiple intelligence reports suggested that an attack was imminent. These warnings came from various sources, including intercepted communications and foreign agents. However, Soviet leader Joseph Stalin remained skeptical, believing that Germany would not risk a two-front war while still fighting Britain. As a result, many preparations were delayed, and Soviet forces were caught off guard when the invasion began. Intelligence also depended on interpretation. Commanders had to decide which reports were reliable and how to act on them. In several cases, assumptions about enemy behavior led leaders to dismiss important information. These early failures demonstrated that intelligence was only as effective as the decisions made from it.

144. Espionage Networks and Secret Agents Across Europe

Alongside codebreaking, espionage played a key role in gathering intelligence. Governments recruited agents to operate behind enemy lines, collecting information about troop movements, industrial production, and political developments. These networks often relied on local resistance groups, who provided knowledge of terrain and conditions. In occupied Europe, resistance movements became an important source of intelligence for the Allies. Members risked arrest or execution to pass on information through coded messages, hidden transmitters, or couriers. Some agents used false identities and lived for months or years within enemy-controlled areas, maintaining contact with intelligence services abroad. However, espionage was extremely dangerous. Many networks were infiltrated or discovered by counterintelligence forces, leading to arrests and executions. Both sides used deception, false information, and double agents to manipulate their opponents. The intelligence war was often invisible, yet it had a direct impact on military operations, as information gathered in secret could influence decisions on the battlefield.

145. The Double-Cross System and Controlled Spies

During the war, British intelligence developed a system that turned enemy spies into controlled sources of information. Known as the Double-Cross System, it involved capturing German agents sent to Britain and persuading them, through cooperation, coercion, or negotiation, to work for the Allies instead. Rather than simply arresting these agents, British intelligence used them to send carefully crafted messages back to Germany.

These messages appeared to provide valuable intelligence, but in reality, they were designed to mislead German command. The system was managed by a specialized group that coordinated what information was sent and ensured that all reports remained consistent. This required careful planning, as even small contradictions could raise suspicion. Over time, the British gained significant control over the flow of intelligence reaching Germany from within the United Kingdom. By managing these agents, they were able to shape enemy expectations and influence strategic decisions without the Germans realizing that their own network had been compromised.

146. Operation Mincemeat and the Use of a False Identity

In 1943, Allied planners needed to mislead German forces about where the next major invasion would take place. The target was Sicily, but if Germany anticipated the attack, it could reinforce the island, making the invasion far more difficult. To distract attention, British intelligence devised a plan to convince the enemy that the invasion would occur elsewhere. The operation involved placing false documents on the body of a man dressed as a British officer. The documents suggested that Allied forces were planning attacks in Greece and Sardinia rather than in Sicily. The body was then released off the coast of Spain, a country that was officially neutral but had contacts with German intelligence. The expectation was that the documents would be recovered and passed on to German authorities. The plan depended on credibility. The identity, personal items, and documents were carefully prepared to appear genuine. When the information reached German command, it contributed to a misinterpretation of Allied intentions, drawing attention away from the actual target.

147. Deception at a Strategic Scale

The success of operations like Mincemeat demonstrated how intelligence could influence entire military campaigns. By shaping what the enemy believed, Allied planners could influence where forces were deployed and how resources were used. In the case of Sicily, German leadership diverted attention and defensive preparations to areas they believed were under threat, reducing their readiness where the actual invasion occurred. This approach was part of a broader strategy that combined multiple forms of deception, including false radio transmissions, misleading reports from double agents, and visible preparations designed to suggest attacks in different locations. Intelligence wasn't only used to gather information but also to create a controlled picture of reality for the enemy. Such operations required careful coordination between intelligence services and military planners. A successful deception could save lives by reducing resistance, while a failure could reveal the strategy and strengthen enemy defenses. By this stage of the war, intelligence had become a central element of planning, shaping decisions long before battles began.

148. Ultra Intelligence and the Battle of the Atlantic

Throughout the war, the Battle of the Atlantic became one of the longest and most critical campaigns, as German submarines, known as U-boats, attempted to cut off supply routes between North America and Britain. These convoys carried food, fuel, and equipment essential to the Allied war effort. If the supply lines failed, Britain's ability to continue the war would be severely weakened. Ultra intelligence, derived from breaking German Enigma codes, played a key role in countering this threat. By intercepting and decrypting German communications, Allied commanders could track the positions of U-boat groups, often referred to as "wolfpacks." This allowed convoys to be rerouted away from danger or escorted more effectively by naval and air forces. However, the use of this intelligence required caution. If the Germans realized their communications were being read, they could change their encryption systems. As a result, commanders sometimes had to allow attacks to proceed rather than reveal the true source of their information. Despite these limitations, Ultra intelligence significantly improved Allied ability to protect shipping and maintain vital supply routes.

149. Codebreaking and the Struggle for Control at Sea

The battle between German submarines and Allied convoys wasn't only fought with ships and aircraft but also with information. As German encryption methods became more complex, codebreakers at Bletchley Park faced periods where they could no longer read enemy messages. During these times, losses at sea increased, showing how closely intelligence was linked to operational success. To regain the advantage, Allied forces worked to capture German equipment, including Enigma machines and codebooks, from damaged or surrendered submarines. These materials provided crucial insight into how the system worked and helped codebreakers restore their ability to read communications. Advances in technology and analysis also improved the speed and accuracy of decryption. Over time, the combination of intelligence, improved convoy systems, and increased air coverage shifted the balance in favor of the

Allies. The ability to understand and anticipate enemy movements reduced losses and strengthened supply lines. The struggle at sea demonstrated that intelligence could be as decisive as firepower, influencing the outcome of an entire campaign.

150. Codebreaking in the Pacific War

In the Pacific, the intelligence war took a different form but was just as critical to survival. The United States focused on breaking Japanese naval codes, particularly a system known as JN-25, which was the primary "operational" code used to coordinate fleet movements. Unlike the mechanical Enigma machine, JN-25 was a book-based cipher. This means that a Japanese officer would first look up a word or phrase in a massive codebook to find a five-digit number and then add a second "random" number to it from a separate table to scramble the message further. American codebreakers, led by Commander Joseph Rochefort in a basement office in Hawaii known as Station HYPO, worked to reconstruct the code using a technique called "traffic analysis." They collected and compared thousands of intercepted radio messages to identify recurring patterns. For example, they realized that certain five-digit groups always appeared at the beginning of messages, which helped them identify the sender's rank or location. Even though the Americans could often decode only 10% to 15% of a message, those fragments were incredibly valuable. By identifying specific code words for geographic locations, which the Americans called "designators," they could estimate where the Japanese fleet was heading. By understanding where Japanese forces would strike next, American commanders could position their carriers for an ambush rather than wandering the empty ocean, turning mathematical analysis into a decisive strategic weapon.

151. Intelligence Warnings Before Pearl Harbor

Before the attack on Pearl Harbor in December 1941, the United States had already intercepted and partially decrypted a number of Japanese communications. These messages indicated rising tensions and suggested that Japan was preparing for major military action. American intelligence was aware that negotiations between the two countries were failing and that conflict was becoming increasingly likely. However, the available information didn't clearly identify where the attack would take place. Many analysts believed that Japan's next move would be directed toward Southeast Asia, where valuable resources such as oil were located. Locations like the Philippines, Malaya, or the Dutch East Indies were considered more likely targets than Hawaii, which was seen as distant and relatively secure. As a result, warnings were general rather than specific. Commanders in the Pacific were advised to remain alert, but the possibility of a direct attack on Pearl Harbor wasn't widely expected. The intelligence existed, but it didn't lead to a clear, immediate defensive response.

152. Misinterpretation, Timing, and Surprise

The failure to prevent the attack on Pearl Harbor wasn't due to a complete lack of information, but rather to how that information was interpreted and acted upon. Intelligence was fragmented across different agencies, and communication between them was limited. Key pieces of information weren't always shared quickly or effectively, leading to gaps in understanding. Timing also played a crucial role. Some intercepted messages suggesting a break in diplomatic relations were decoded only hours before the attack, leaving little time to respond. Even when warnings were sent, they often arrived too late or lacked enough detail to prompt immediate action. In addition, existing assumptions influenced decision-making. Many believed that a surprise attack on a distant naval base would be too risky for Japan. This underestimation contributed to a lack of preparedness. When the attack began on December 7, 1941, it achieved tactical surprise, demonstrating how intelligence can fail not only through absence but also through misinterpretation, delay, and misplaced confidence.

153. The Manhattan Project and Secret Science

The groundwork for a nuclear program in the United States began as early as late 1939, following a letter from Albert Einstein to President Roosevelt warning that Nazi Germany might be developing "extremely powerful bombs of a new type." However, it wasn't until August 1942 that the effort was officially organized as the Manhattan Project, a massive undertaking led by the U.S. Army Corps of Engineers under General Leslie Groves and scientific director J. Robert Oppenheimer. The goal was to harness nuclear fission, the process of splitting an atom's nucleus to release a massive amount of energy, to create a weapon of unprecedented destructive power. The project brought together scientists, engineers, and military personnel from the United States, Britain, and Canada, driven by the intense fear that Germany might achieve a nuclear breakthrough first. The scale of the project was staggering, employing over 130,000 people and costing nearly $2 billion (equivalent to roughly $35 billion today). To maintain the highest level of security, entire "secret cities" were built from scratch in remote locations. In Oak Ridge, Tennessee, massive plants used electromagnetism and gas to separate Uranium-235, the fuel needed for the bomb. Meanwhile, in Hanford, Washington, the first full-scale nuclear reactors were built to produce plutonium, an even more powerful man-made element. The actual design and assembly of the weapons took place at a central laboratory in Los Alamos, New Mexico. To protect the secret, the military used compartmentalization: a security method in which workers are given only the specific information needed for their individual tasks. Most employees at Oak Ridge had no idea they were working on a weapon; they simply monitored gauges in massive factories, unaware of the final product. Even Harry S. Truman was kept in the dark about the project until he became president in April 1945. The effort reached its climax on July 16, 1945, in the New Mexico desert with the Trinity Test, the first successful detonation of a nuclear device. The explosion was equal to roughly 21,000 tons of TNT, turning the desert sand into green glass. While the project was born from the threat of Nazi Germany, the successful test occurred months after Germany's surrender, leaving the United States with a weapon that would instead be used to end the war in the Pacific.

154. Espionage and Secrets Within the Atomic Program

Despite the strict security surrounding the Manhattan Project, information about it wasn't completely contained. Soviet intelligence managed to place agents within the program, allowing them to gather details about the development of atomic weapons. These agents passed information to the Soviet Union, providing insights that would later assist in its own nuclear program. The structure of the project, with its many sites and large workforce, posed security challenges. While most participants had limited knowledge of the overall effort, some individuals had access to critical information. Intelligence services on both sides recognized the importance of scientific developments, and efforts were made to gather or protect knowledge wherever possible. The presence of espionage within the project showed that even the most secret programs were vulnerable. Information gathered during the war contributed to the rapid development of nuclear weapons by multiple countries in the years that followed. The intelligence dimension of the Manhattan Project extended its impact beyond the war itself, shaping the balance of power in the postwar world.

155. Operation Fortitude and the Illusion of Invasion

In the months leading up to the Allied invasion of Western Europe in 1944, planners recognized that surprise would be critical. If German forces could be convinced that the main landing would occur somewhere other than the actual target, they might delay sending reinforcements, giving Allied troops time to establish a foothold. To achieve this, the Allies launched a large-scale deception plan known as Operation Fortitude. This operation was designed to mislead German intelligence about both the location and timing of the invasion. The real landing would take place in Normandy, on the northern coast of France, but Fortitude aimed to convince German commanders that the main attack would occur at the Pas-de-Calais, the narrowest point between Britain and France. This location appeared more logical because it was closer to England and offered shorter supply lines. To reinforce the deception, Allied forces generated false radio traffic, planted misleading intelligence, and used double agents to pass carefully constructed information to the Germans. These agents, some of whom were under Allied control, reported the buildup of forces in southeastern England, creating the impression that a major invasion force was waiting there. Over time, these efforts shaped German expectations, causing them to prepare for an attack in the wrong place.

156. The Creation of a Phantom Army

A key part of Operation Fortitude was the creation of an entirely fictional military formation known as the First United States Army Group (FUSAG). This "army" existed only on paper, but it was presented to German intelligence as a powerful force preparing for invasion. To make the illusion convincing, the Allies used a combination of physical props, signals, and controlled information. Inflatable tanks and aircraft were placed in fields to simulate large concentrations of equipment. Wooden structures and dummy landing craft were constructed along the coast. Meanwhile, radio operators transmitted messages that mimicked the communications of a real army, complete with the patterns and terminology expected by enemy listeners. Even the movement of units was staged to suggest training exercises and preparations for an imminent attack. The deception was further strengthened by placing General George Patton, one of the Allies' most well-known commanders, in charge of the fictitious army. German leaders considered him one of the most capable Allied generals, so his supposed involvement added credibility to the threat. As a result, even after the real invasion began in Normandy in June 1944,

German forces continued to expect a larger attack at Pas-de-Calais and held back key divisions. This delay played a crucial role in the success of the Allied landings.

157. Intelligence and the Normandy Breakout

After the Allied landings in Normandy on June 6, 1944, intelligence continued to play a decisive role in the next phase of the campaign. While German commanders initially believed the Normandy landings were a diversion, intercepted communications and reconnaissance began to reveal the true scale of the Allied buildup. However, by the time this realization spread, the delay caused by earlier deception operations had already weakened German responses. Allied intelligence units worked closely with resistance groups across France, who provided real-time information about German troop movements, supply lines, and defensive positions. These reports were transmitted through coded radio messages and helped Allied commanders plan attacks with greater precision. At the same time, Ultra intelligence from decrypted German communications revealed how German units were being redeployed, allowing Allied forces to anticipate counterattacks. One of the key moments came in late July 1944 during Operation Cobra, the Allied "breakout" from the coastal areas of Normandy. After weeks of being stuck in the dense French countryside, the Allies used a combination of three intelligence tools to shatter the deadlock: aerial reconnaissance (photos taken by planes flying overhead), intercepted communications (radio messages decoded by experts), and resistance reports (secret information sent by French citizens fighting against the occupation). By layering this information together, Allied planners identified exactly where the German defensive line was at its weakest. Using these insights, the Allies launched a massive, concentrated attack on those specific thin spots. This allowed their armored divisions to punch through the German front and finally begin racing across the open plains of France toward Paris.

158. The July Plot and Intelligence Inside Germany

In July 1944, one of the most dramatic intelligence-related events of the war came from within Germany itself. A group of German military officers and officials, convinced that the war was lost and that Hitler's leadership was leading the country to destruction, organized a plan to assassinate him and take control of the government. This plan became known as the July Plot. The central figure in the operation was Colonel Claus von Stauffenberg, who placed a bomb in a briefcase during a meeting at Hitler's headquarters in East Prussia on July 20, 1944. The explosion killed several people, but Hitler survived with relatively minor injuries. The failure of the assassination attempt led to a rapid crackdown by the Nazi regime. Although not an intelligence operation in the traditional sense, the plot revealed the extent of internal dissent within Germany and the limits of control even in a highly authoritarian system. German intelligence services, including the Gestapo, launched extensive investigations to uncover those involved. Thousands were arrested, and many were executed. The event demonstrated that even as Germany maintained strict control over information, resistance existed within its own leadership. It also highlighted that intelligence wasn't used only against external enemies but also to monitor and suppress internal opposition.

159. The Ardennes Offensive and Intelligence Misjudgment

In December 1944, Germany launched a surprise counteroffensive in the Ardennes forest region of Belgium and Luxembourg, an operation that became known as the Battle of the Bulge. The goal was to split Allied forces and capture the vital port of Antwerp. Despite the extensive intelligence capabilities of the Allies, the attack achieved a significant degree of surprise. German forces maintained strict radio silence and used landlines instead of wireless communication, limiting the amount of information available for interception. Troop movements were carried out under the cover of bad weather and dense forest, reducing the effectiveness of aerial reconnaissance. As a result, many Allied analysts believed that Germany no longer had the strength to launch a major offensive. There were warning signs. Some intelligence reports suggested unusual German activity, but these were often dismissed or interpreted as defensive preparations rather than an offensive threat. When the attack began on December 16, 1944, it initially caught Allied forces off guard, leading to heavy fighting and temporary gains for German troops. However, once the scale of the attack became clear, Allied intelligence and logistics helped coordinate a response. Improved weather allowed air support, and intercepted communications revealed German supply shortages. Within weeks, the offensive was contained and eventually pushed back. The battle showed that even advanced intelligence systems could fail when assumptions influenced interpretation.

160. Soviet Intelligence and the Final Offensive

As the war moved into its final phase in early 1945, Soviet intelligence played a key role in preparing large-scale offensives against German forces.

The Red Army gathered information through reconnaissance units, partisan networks, and intercepted communications, building a detailed picture of German defenses along the Eastern Front. One of the most important operations was the Vistula–Oder Offensive, launched in January 1945. Soviet planners used intelligence to identify weak points in German lines and to concentrate overwhelming force at specific locations. Deception was also used to conceal the true scale and timing of the attack, preventing German forces from reinforcing critical sectors. When the offensive began, Soviet forces advanced rapidly across Poland, pushing German units back toward the Oder River, only about forty-three miles (seventy kilometers) from Berlin. The speed of the advance shocked German commanders, many of whom had underestimated Soviet capabilities. Intelligence allowed Soviet forces to coordinate massive troop movements and maintain momentum, ensuring that German defenses couldn't recover.

161. Intelligence and the Race for Berlin

In early 1945, as Allied forces closed in on Germany from both the west and the east, intelligence played a key role in shaping the final advance toward Berlin. Both the Western Allies and the Soviet Union gathered information on German troop positions, defensive lines, and supply conditions, but their strategic goals differed. While the Soviets aimed to capture Berlin, Western Allied leaders prioritized avoiding unnecessary casualties and securing other key regions. Soviet intelligence, supported by reconnaissance units and partisan networks, provided detailed information about German defenses around the capital. This allowed Soviet commanders to plan a massive offensive involving multiple army groups, designed to overwhelm German positions through sheer force and coordination. At the same time, intercepted communications revealed the weakening state of German units, many of which were understrength and poorly supplied. In the west, Allied intelligence suggested that German resistance was collapsing unevenly, with some units surrendering while others continued to fight. This influenced decisions about where to advance and where to halt. Ultimately, the Western Allies stopped short of Berlin, allowing Soviet forces to take the city. Intelligence, in this case, didn't just guide military movements; it also shaped political decisions about how the war would end.

162. The Collapse of German Communications

By the final months of the war, Germany's ability to coordinate its forces had been severely weakened. Continuous bombing campaigns had destroyed railways, communication lines, and industrial centers, making it increasingly difficult for orders to reach front-line units. At the same time, Allied interception of German communications meant that many messages were no longer secure. German commanders often relied on outdated information or incomplete reports, leading to confusion and ineffective decisions. In some cases, units received orders to attack or hold positions that had already been lost. The breakdown of communication networks also made coordination among different parts of the German military increasingly difficult. Allied intelligence, on the other hand, became more effective as the war progressed. Intercepted messages, aerial reconnaissance, and reports from advancing troops provided a clearer picture of the battlefield. This allowed Allied commanders to identify weak points and exploit them quickly. The contrast between the two sides was stark. While the Allies were improving their ability to gather and use information, Germany was losing control over its own communication systems. This imbalance contributed to the rapid collapse of German defenses in 1945, as the ability to command and coordinate forces is essential in any military operation. Without it, even large armies can become disorganized and ineffective.

163. Intelligence and the Atomic Decision

As the war in Europe ended, intelligence also influenced decisions in the Pacific. American leaders were trying to determine how to bring the war with Japan to a close, and one key question was whether Japan would surrender without a full-scale invasion. Through intercepted Japanese communications, particularly diplomatic messages, American intelligence gained insight into Japan's internal debates. These messages suggested that some Japanese leaders were seeking a negotiated settlement, but others were committed to continuing the war. The information indicated that Japan was divided but not yet ready to accept unconditional surrender. At the same time, intelligence estimates predicted that an invasion of the Japanese mainland could result in extremely high casualties for both sides. These projections were based on previous battles, in which Japanese forces had fought to the last, and on reports about preparations to defend the home islands. This combination of intelligence, showing both Japan's willingness to resist and the potential cost of invasion, contributed to the decision to use atomic weapons. While not the only factor, intelligence played a role in shaping how American leaders understood their options, influencing one of the most significant decisions of the war.

164. Intelligence and the Soviet Entry into the Pacific War

Another crucial factor in the final phase of the war was the planned entry of the Soviet Union into the conflict against Japan. This decision had been agreed upon earlier by Allied leaders, but its timing and execution were closely tied to intelligence assessments. Soviet intelligence had been monitoring Japanese forces in Manchuria, where a large army was stationed. These forces were considered significant, but intelligence also suggested that they were overstretched and not fully prepared for a major offensive. Meanwhile, American intelligence recognized that a Soviet attack could further pressure Japan and accelerate the end of the war. In August 1945, shortly after the atomic bombings, the Soviet Union launched a massive offensive into Manchuria. Using detailed intelligence and overwhelming force, Soviet troops advanced rapidly, defeating Japanese forces in a matter of weeks. The speed of the offensive surprised many observers and demonstrated the effectiveness of coordinated planning. The combination of atomic attacks and the Soviet invasion created a situation in which Japanese leaders faced multiple threats at once. Intelligence on both sides helped shape these final operations, contributing to the decisions that ultimately ended the war.

165. The Lasting Impact of Wartime Intelligence

The intelligence operations of World War II had a lasting impact far beyond the conflict itself. During the war, countries developed new methods for gathering, analyzing, and protecting information, including codebreaking, signal interception, and large-scale deception. These methods proved so effective that they became permanent parts of national security systems after the war ended. Organizations created for wartime intelligence, such as codebreaking centers and cryptographic units, laid the foundation for modern intelligence agencies. Techniques developed during the war influenced how governments approached surveillance, espionage, and information security in the decades that followed. The importance of secrecy and information control became central to global politics. The war also demonstrated that intelligence could be as decisive as military strength. The ability to understand enemy plans, protect one's own communications, and influence what the enemy believed could shape entire campaigns. This realization contributed to the emergence of new forms of conflict after the war, where intelligence and information would play a central role. In this sense, World War II wasn't only a conflict of armies and weapons but also a turning point in how information itself became a powerful tool of war.

FOUR

Spies, Agents, and Double Lives

World War II created a world in which secrecy and deception became essential tools of survival and strategy. Spies operated across borders, gathering information, sabotaging operations, and influencing events from the shadows. Many lived double lives, navigating constant danger where a single mistake could mean capture or death. This chapter looks at the individuals who operated in this hidden world, including agents sent behind enemy lines, resistance fighters working in occupied territories, and the networks that supported them. It reveals the risks they faced and the crucial role they played in shaping the course of the war. It was a conflict where some of the most important battles were fought without uniforms, in silence, and far from the front lines.

166. The Cambridge Five and the Quiet Infiltration

In the 1930s, a group of students at Cambridge University in Britain began making decisions that would have long-term consequences for the intelligence war that followed. Influenced by the political climate of the time, including economic instability and the rise of fascism across Europe, several of them became sympathetic to communist ideas. Soviet intelligence identified their potential early and recruited them while they were still students, before they entered government service. Over the following years, these individuals, later known as the "Cambridge Five," moved into influential positions within British institutions, including intelligence agencies and the diplomatic corps. Because they came from trusted backgrounds and appeared loyal, they weren't initially suspected. This allowed them to pass sensitive information to the Soviet Union over an extended period. Their actions provided insight into Allied planning and intelligence operations, showing that espionage wasn't only carried out across borders but also from within. The group remained active for years, demonstrating how long-term infiltration could shape the intelligence landscape of the war.

167. Richard Sorge and the Warning from Tokyo

In the years leading up to and during the early stages of World War II, one of the most effective intelligence sources for the Soviet Union was operating in Japan. Richard Sorge, a German journalist and committed communist, worked secretly as a Soviet agent while maintaining close connections with German diplomats and Japanese officials. His position gave him access to information that was difficult for others to obtain. In 1941, Sorge reported that Germany was preparing to invade the Soviet Union, providing an early warning of Operation Barbarossa. Later that year, he delivered another critical message: Japan didn't intend to attack the Soviet Union in the near future. This information allowed the Soviet leadership to move experienced divisions from Siberia to the western front, where they were needed to defend Moscow. These reinforcements played an important role in slowing the German advance during the winter of 1941. Sorge's work demonstrated how intelligence gathered far from the battlefield could influence key decisions. However, Japanese authorities became suspicious after intercepting coded radio transmissions linked to his network, and the arrest of one of his associates led investigators to him. He was eventually arrested by Japanese authorities and later executed, with his contributions becoming widely recognized only after the war.

168. Duško Popov and the Warning That Went Unheeded

In the early years of the war, espionage often depended on individuals who lived double lives, constantly balancing trust and suspicion. One such figure was Duško Popov, a Yugoslav double agent who worked for British intelligence while pretending to serve Germany. His role required him to travel across Europe and the United States, maintaining contact with German handlers while secretly reporting back to the Allies. In 1941, Popov was sent to the United States by German intelligence with a detailed questionnaire about American military installations. Among the locations mentioned was Pearl Harbor, the major U.S. naval base in Hawaii. Recognizing the significance of these questions, Popov passed the information to American authorities, hoping it would raise concern. However, his warning didn't lead to a decisive response. Part of the problem was that intelligence agencies were cautious about trusting information from double agents, whose reliability was always uncertain. Popov himself operated under constant pressure, knowing that a single mistake could expose his role and lead to execution. His experience illustrated one of the key challenges of espionage: even accurate intelligence could be overlooked if it didn't fit existing expectations or if its source wasn't fully trusted.

169. The Abwehr and the Limits of German Espionage

Germany entered the war with its own intelligence organization, the Abwehr, responsible for espionage and counterintelligence operations. However, despite early efforts, the Abwehr struggled to build effective networks, particularly in Britain. Many of the agents it sent were quickly identified, captured, or turned by British intelligence, often within days of arrival. For individual spies, this meant entering an environment where survival was unlikely. Agents were dropped into unfamiliar territory, often with limited support and little local knowledge. Some were betrayed, while others made small mistakes that exposed them. Once captured, they faced interrogation, imprisonment, or execution. The weaknesses of the Abwehr weren't only operational but also internal. Rivalries between different intelligence organizations, as well as distrust within the Nazi system, made coordination difficult. Some officers within the Abwehr even secretly opposed Hitler, creating further instability. For the individuals involved, espionage was rarely glamorous. It was a dangerous and uncertain existence, where loyalty, deception, and survival were constantly in tension. The failure of German intelligence networks in places like Britain showed how difficult it was to operate successfully in hostile territory, especially when the enemy was already watching closely.

170. Virginia Hall and the Limping Lady

One of the most effective Allied agents operating in occupied Europe was Virginia Hall, an American who worked with British intelligence and later the United States. Her presence in the field was unusual for another reason: she had a prosthetic leg, which she nicknamed "Cuthbert," after losing her lower leg in an accident years earlier. Despite this, she volunteered for one of the most dangerous roles in the war. Operating in France after its occupation by Germany, Hall built networks of resistance fighters, organized supply drops, and helped coordinate sabotage operations. She also assisted downed Allied airmen, guiding them through escape routes out of occupied territory. Her work required constant movement and secrecy, often traveling long distances on foot or by bicycle, even with her disability. The Gestapo, Germany's secret police, became aware of her activities and referred to her as "the most dangerous of all Allied spies." Her physical condition, which might have been seen as a limitation, actually became part of her disguise, allowing her to blend in as an ordinary civilian. When her network was compromised, she was forced to flee across the Pyrenees Mountains into Spain in the winter, a difficult journey even for a fully able-bodied person. Hall later returned to France, continuing her work under even greater risk.

171. Noor Inayat Khan and the Silent Radio

In occupied France, one of the most dangerous roles in the resistance was that of a wireless operator. These agents were responsible for transmitting coded messages back to Britain, often from within enemy territory. Because radio signals could be detected, German forces used tracking equipment to locate transmissions, meaning that operators had to move frequently and limit how long they stayed on the air. Many were captured within weeks. Noor Inayat Khan, a British agent of Indian origin, was sent into France in 1943 as a radio operator. After a series of arrests destroyed much of her network, she became one of the last remaining operators in the region. Despite the risk, she continued transmitting messages, knowing that her signals were essential for coordinating resistance activities and supply drops. Living under constant threat, she moved from place to place, carrying her radio equipment and avoiding detection. Eventually, she was betrayed and captured by German forces. Even under interrogation, she refused to provide useful information and attempted escape more than once. Because she was considered highly dangerous, she was classified as a "night and fog" prisoner, a category for those who were to disappear without a trace. Noor Inayat Khan was later executed in 1944. Her story highlighted the extreme risks faced by agents in the field, where communication itself could reveal their location and where even silence under interrogation required extraordinary resilience.

172. Juan Pujol and the Imaginary Network

One of the most unusual spies of the war was Juan Pujol, a Spanish civilian who had no formal training in intelligence but was determined to fight against Nazi Germany. At first, he tried to offer his services to the British, but when they rejected him, he decided to act on his own. Posing as a pro-

German sympathizer, he convinced German intelligence to recruit him as a spy. Without ever setting foot in Britain, Pujol began sending reports to Germany based entirely on information gathered from newspapers, maps, and public sources. To make his reports appear more credible, he invented an entire network of fictional agents across Britain, each with their own personalities, backgrounds, and roles. Over time, he built a detailed imaginary organization that German intelligence believed was real. Eventually, British intelligence discovered his activities and decided to recruit him as a double agent, giving him the codename "Garbo." From that point on, his false network became a powerful tool of deception. He continued to send reports to Germany, mixing harmless truths with carefully crafted misinformation. By the time of the D-Day invasion in 1944, Pujol's network had become one of Germany's most trusted sources. His messages helped convince German commanders that the main Allied invasion would take place away from Normandy, causing them to delay sending reinforcements. Pujol later received awards from both sides, honored by Germany for his "service" and by Britain for his role in the Allied victory, making him one of the few spies to be decorated by opposing forces.

173. Nancy Wake and the Most Wanted Woman in France

Nancy Wake was one of the most active and widely pursued Allied agents operating in occupied France. Originally from New Zealand and later working for British intelligence, she became deeply involved in resistance activities, coordinating sabotage operations and helping Allied forces disrupt German control. Known by the Gestapo as "The White Mouse" because of her ability to evade capture, Wake constantly moved between safe houses, carrying messages, organizing fighters, and helping supply networks operate under occupation. She worked closely with resistance groups, helping them receive weapons, explosives, and instructions dropped by air from Britain. Her work required both physical endurance and constant awareness. At one point, after a communications breakdown, she reportedly cycled over 185 miles (about 300 kilometers) through enemy territory to reestablish contact with her network. Throughout her missions, she lived under the constant threat of arrest, knowing that capture would likely lead to interrogation and execution. Despite being one of the most wanted individuals in France, she managed to survive the war. Her story reflects the scale of civilian involvement in intelligence work, where ordinary individuals took on extraordinary risks, operating in secrecy while contributing directly to military operations.

174. Cicero and the Spy Inside the Embassy

One of the most unusual intelligence breaches of the war took place not on a battlefield but inside the British Embassy in Ankara, Turkey, a country that remained officially neutral for much of the conflict. The man at the center of it was Elyesa Bazna, a valet who worked for the British ambassador. Using his position inside the embassy, he gained access to highly sensitive documents, including reports and diplomatic communications. At night, when the building was quiet, Bazna would secretly open safes, photograph documents, and then return everything to its place before morning. He sold these photographs to German intelligence, which gave him the codename "Cicero." The information he provided included details about Allied planning and discussions, making him one of the most valuable sources the Germans had at the time. However, his story also showed the limits of intelligence. Some German officials distrusted the material, suspecting it might be a British deception, while others failed to act on it effectively. As a result, even though the information was genuine, it didn't always produce the strategic advantage it might have offered. For Bazna, the work was driven partly by money and partly by opportunity, but it carried enormous risk. Had he been discovered, he would likely have been executed. His actions revealed how espionage could occur in unexpected places, where access and timing mattered as much as ideology or loyalty.

175. Odette Sansom and Resistance Under Interrogation

For many agents, the greatest danger came not during their missions, but after capture. Odette Sansom, a British agent working in occupied France, experienced this reality firsthand. She had been sent to help coordinate resistance networks, passing information and supporting operations behind enemy lines. In 1943, she was arrested by German forces after her network was compromised. Following her capture, Odette was subjected to interrogation by the Gestapo. Like many captured agents, she was pressured to reveal information about resistance networks, contacts, and operations. Instead, she attempted to mislead her captors, claiming she was married to a high-ranking British officer, hoping this would make the Germans treat her as a more valuable prisoner rather than execute her immediately. She endured severe treatment, including physical abuse, but refused to provide useful intelligence. Her resistance under interrogation helped protect other members of her network from exposure. Eventually, she was sent to a concentration camp, where conditions were harsh, and survival was uncertain. Odette survived the war, but her experience reflected the reality faced by many agents. Espionage didn't end with capture. For those who were caught, the struggle often continued in interrogation rooms and prison camps, where silence itself became an act of resistance.

176. The Lucy Spy Ring and Intelligence from Within

One of the most mysterious and valuable intelligence networks of the war operated out of neutral Switzerland and became known as the "Lucy Spy Ring." The central figure, Rudolf Roessler, was a German exile who maintained contacts with individuals inside the German military and political system. Through these connections, he received detailed information about German plans, troop movements, and upcoming operations. What made this network unusual was the level of detail and the speed at which information arrived. Reports often reached the Soviet Union with remarkable accuracy, sometimes even before orders had fully been implemented on the battlefield. This intelligence was passed through intermediaries using coded radio transmissions, eventually reaching Soviet commanders. The exact source of Roessler's information remained unclear even after the war. Some believed it came from high-ranking officers who opposed Hitler, while others suspected that parts of the information may have been indirectly influenced by other intelligence operations. Regardless of its origin, the intelligence proved valuable in several campaigns, helping Soviet forces prepare for German actions. For those involved, the risks were extreme. Operating across borders, relying on secret contacts, and transmitting sensitive information meant that discovery could lead to execution. The Lucy Spy Ring demonstrated that some of the most important intelligence didn't come from agents behind enemy lines but from individuals within the enemy's own system.

177. Violette Szabo and the Final Stand

Violette Szabo was one of many agents sent into occupied France to support resistance operations, but her missions placed her in some of the most dangerous situations of the war. Working with British intelligence, she was responsible for coordinating local resistance groups, organizing sabotage, and maintaining communication with Allied command. During her second mission in 1944, shortly after the D-Day landings, Szabo was dropped into central France to help disrupt German movements. At one point, while traveling with resistance fighters, her group was stopped by German forces. Realizing that escape was necessary, she took up a defensive position with a submachine gun, providing covering fire so that others could attempt to flee. She fought until she ran out of ammunition and was eventually captured. Following her arrest, she was interrogated but refused to provide information about her network. She was later deported to a concentration camp, where she was executed in 1945. Szabo's story reflected the reality faced by many agents operating in occupied territories. Missions were often brief, intense, and carried out under constant threat. Capture could come suddenly, and survival was never guaranteed. In many cases, agents continued to resist even after their missions had ended, demonstrating that espionage required not only skill but also extraordinary personal courage.

FIVE

The Soldier

At the center of World War II were the soldiers who fought on its many fronts. They endured extreme conditions, from the frozen winters of the Eastern Front to the heat of desert campaigns and the dense terrain of jungle warfare. For many, survival depended on discipline, resilience, and the ability to adapt to constantly changing circumstances. This chapter examines the experiences of those who served, including the realities of combat, the challenges of daily life in the military, and the psychological toll of prolonged warfare. It explores the human dimension of the conflict, focusing on the individuals who carried out orders and faced the direct consequences of the war. It was a war fought not only by nations but also by individuals whose endurance shaped its outcome.

178. Mobilization and the Call to Arms in Europe

In the late summer of 1939, European nations mobilized with a speed that shocked civilian populations. In France, over six million men were called up in just a few weeks. In Germany, the system was even more efficient; by the time they invaded Poland, the *Wehrmacht* (German Defense Force) had 3.7 million men under arms. Unlike the United States' later peacetime draft, most major powers in Europe already had systems of conscription in place. Countries such as Germany, France, and the Soviet Union required young men to register for military service, and in times of crisis, these systems allowed governments to call up large numbers of reservists almost immediately. Many soldiers had already completed basic training during earlier periods of service but had returned to civilian life. Mobilization meant being recalled, sometimes with only a few days' notice, leaving behind jobs, families, and unfinished lives. The transition was abrupt. In Britain, the "calling up" of reservists meant that a man could be working in a bank on Friday and, by Monday, be in uniform, learning to fire a Lee-Enfield rifle. This early period (September 1939 to May 1940) became known as the "Phoney War" or *Sitzkrieg* (Sitting War), where soldiers sat in the Maginot Line or the Siegfried Line, dealing with boredom and mud rather than bullets. The process of recruitment and selection varied by country. Some men were assigned based on age, physical condition, and prior experience, while others were placed where manpower was most urgently needed. Not all were sent directly to combat roles. Some were assigned to engineering units, transport services, or support roles essential to sustaining armies. Despite this structure, mobilization often felt rushed and disorganized. Equipment shortages were common, particularly in the early months, and not all units were fully prepared. For many, the transition from civilian life to military service was abrupt, marked by uncertainty about how long the war would last and what their role would be.

179. Training, Equipment, and the First Days in Uniform

Once mobilized, soldiers entered a period of training intended to prepare them for combat, though the available time varied widely. A typical soldier's burden was staggering, as they were required to carry everything needed for survival on their backs. A British soldier's "Full Marching Order" weighed about sixty pounds (twenty-seven kilograms), while a German *Landser* (infantryman) carried nearly seventy pounds (thirty-two kilograms). This weight included the standard rifle, most of which were bolt-action designs, such as the German Karabiner 98k or the Soviet Mosin-Nagant, which required the soldier to manually cycle a bolt after every shot. Training emphasized discipline in the smallest details: keeping boots greased, packing gear to balance the load, and maintaining weapons amid mud and dust. These routines weren't only practical but also helped create a sense of order and control in a vast military system where soldiers often understood little about the larger strategy or the intensity of the combat that lay ahead.

180. "Fit," "Deferred," or Rejected: The U.S. Peacetime Draft and Mass Screening

Before the United States entered combat, Washington began building an army through the Selective Training and Service Act, signed on September

16, 1940: the first U.S. peacetime draft. Men were registered, classified, and either called up, deferred, or rejected. What made this system feel personal wasn't the law; it was the examination line. Induction centers ran recruits through medical and sometimes psychiatric screening that could be invasive and humiliating, with doctors deciding if someone was "fit" for combat, better suited for support work, or unfit entirely. Standards also shifted as manpower demands grew: early strictness could keep out men for issues like poor eyesight or dental problems, but by 1942, the military increasingly accepted "fixable" problems through treatments (glasses, dental work, etc.) because the war was expanding faster than ideal recruitment pools. Meanwhile, classification wasn't just a bureaucracy; it shaped lives: some men felt stigma if rejected, others felt guilt if deferred while friends shipped out, and many entered service convinced it would be brief, until the war made "brief" impossible.

181. Segregated Service and Fighting Two Wars at Once

After the Selective Training and Service Act was introduced by the United States, Black Americans were both allowed and pressured to serve, but they entered a military that was rigidly segregated, meaning Black and white soldiers were kept in separate units and lived in separate housing. Training bases often mirrored the "Jim Crow" laws of the era, which enforced racial separation and meant that Black recruits faced routine harassment and were often restricted to manual labor instead of being given combat roles. This created a bitter contradiction: men were being asked to fight against fascism (a system of government that suppresses freedom) in Europe while they were being treated as second-class citizens in their own country. In 1942, Black newspapers and civil rights leaders launched the Double V Campaign. The "Two Vs" stood for Victory over enemies abroad and Victory over racism at home. This movement encouraged Black Americans to serve their country while simultaneously demanding the full rights of citizenship they were fighting to protect. As the need for more soldiers grew, new opportunities slowly opened up. Specialized units proved their skill in battle, such as the Tuskegee Airmen, the first Black military pilots, who flew dangerous escort missions over the Mediterranean. On the ground, the 761st Tank Battalion (known as the "Black Panthers") entered combat in 1944 and earned high praise for their bravery in the face of the enemy. For these soldiers, the war was a "double struggle," surviving the dangers of the battlefield while carrying the added burden of serving a system that demanded their sacrifice while still questioning their humanity.

182. Orders, Ranks, and the Invisible Structure of Command

Once a civilian entered military service, he became part of a vast structure that extended far beyond the battlefield. The army was organized as a clear hierarchy, designed to control large numbers of men across different fronts and conditions. At the lowest level was the private, responsible for carrying out orders, maintaining equipment, and functioning as part of a small unit. Around ten to twelve soldiers formed a squad, led by a corporal or sergeant, who was often the most direct authority a soldier experienced. Several squads formed a platoon under a lieutenant, while multiple platoons made up a company commanded by a captain. These companies combined into battalions and regiments, and eventually into divisions, corps, and entire armies, each level increasing in size, distance from the front, and responsibility. Above the battlefield, command became more strategic. Generals coordinated movements across entire regions, while national headquarters planned campaigns that could involve millions of soldiers. Civilian leaders, such as presidents or prime ministers, formally held ultimate authority, deciding overall war aims and approving major operations. This structure was designed to create order, ensuring that instructions could be passed from the highest level down to individual soldiers. However, communication wasn't always smooth. Orders could be delayed, misunderstood, or based on outdated information. A decision made far from the front might not reflect the reality on the ground. For soldiers, the system often felt distant and abstract. Most never saw beyond their immediate officers, yet their actions were shaped by a chain of command that stretched far above them, connecting individual experience to the larger direction of the war.

183. Uniforms, Helmets, and the Limits of Protection

A soldier's uniform was designed for function rather than comfort, serving as his only shelter and shield against both the enemy and the elements. Standard issue typically included a wool jacket, trousers, boots, a helmet, and webbing, a system of canvas straps and belts used to carry ammunition, water, and tools. While these items offered some protection, they were limited in what they could do; for instance, steel helmets, such as the German Stahlhelm or the American M1, were mainly designed to protect the head from shrapnel (small, jagged metal fragments from explosions) and falling debris rather than direct gunfire at close range. Boots were perhaps the most critical piece of equipment a soldier owned, as poor foot care could take a man out of action faster than a bullet. Long marches, wet conditions, and freezing weather made specialized footwear essential, from the hobnailed Ammo Boots of the British to the high-topped jackboots of the German infantry. However, uniforms had to adapt to environments they weren't always designed for, such as the thin cotton "drill" uniforms issued to the Afrika Korps for the desert or the thick, padded Telogreika jackets worn by Soviet troops to survive the Siberian cold. Because supplies weren't always consistent, soldiers frequently modified their clothing by adding layers of newspaper for insulation, cutting fabric to make improvised gloves, or using captured enemy gear, like the highly prized Soviet fur caps, to improve their chances of survival. Over time, uniforms became worn, patched, and encrusted with the mud of the front, reflecting the brutal conditions of service. Protection remained partial at best, and every soldier understood that while his equipment could help deflect a piece of rubble or a distant fragment, it offered no guarantee of survival against the heavy machinery of modern war.

184. Bread Bags, Field Kitchens, and the Reality of Rations

As armies began to move, soldiers quickly learned that food was the engine of the army, essential for maintaining both the physical strength and the morale needed to continue fighting. When supply lines functioned properly, meals were prepared by field kitchens, which followed units to provide hot food such as soup, stew, or coffee; German soldiers even nicknamed their horse-drawn field kitchen the "Goulash Cannon" (*Gulaschkanone*). These hot meals offered a brief, precious sense of normal life, but during rapid advances or retreats, these kitchens often couldn't reach the front, forcing soldiers to rely on iron rations and whatever they could carry in small bags attached to their equipment. The composition of these rations varied by nation: American troops primarily used the C-Ration, a heavy canned meal of meat and beans, or the K-Ration, a lighter, waxed-paper pack designed for paratroopers, while in the Soviet Red Army, the staple was *kasha* (a thick buckwheat porridge) and a heavy, dark rye bread that was often so hard it had to be soaked in soup just to be edible. Beyond food, water remained an ongoing concern; canteens often ran dry, and when clean sources were unavailable, soldiers were forced to drink from rivers, puddles, or melted snow, which frequently led to debilitating illnesses. To supplement these meager supplies, troops often gathered local resources, took food from farms, or traded with civilians, because food was ultimately more than just sustenance: it was a psychological lifeline, and the memory of intense hunger stayed with them as clearly as the battles themselves.

185. Cold, Mud, and the Return of Trench Conditions

Although World War II is often remembered for fast-moving battles, many soldiers found themselves in conditions that resembled the trench warfare of the previous war. As fighting slowed in certain areas, especially during the winter months of 1939–1940, troops were forced to dig defensive positions and remain in place for extended periods. These positions were often little more than shallow foxholes or hastily constructed trenches. Rain turned the ground into thick mud that clung to boots and soaked clothing. In colder regions, water froze overnight, making movement difficult and increasing the risk of frostbite. Soldiers slept in these conditions. often without proper shelter, using blankets or whatever materials they could find for protection. Keeping dry became nearly impossible. Wet clothing led to skin infections and "trench foot," a painful condition caused by prolonged exposure to moisture and cold. These environments were physically and mentally exhausting. Soldiers had to remain alert for enemy attacks while dealing with discomfort that never fully went away.

186. The First Encounter with Combat

For many soldiers, the transition from training to combat was sudden and disorienting. Days or weeks of marching could end in moments of violence that felt overwhelming and difficult to process. The first experience of combat was often confusing rather than dramatic. Visibility was limited, orders were shouted or misunderstood, and the source of danger wasn't always clear. Gunfire could come from unseen positions, and explosions could occur without warning. Many soldiers later described their first engagement as chaotic and fragmented. Some focused on simple tasks, loading a weapon, following a command, and staying close to others while trying to manage fear. Training provided basic instructions, but it couldn't fully prepare individuals for the noise, speed, and unpredictability of real combat. Reactions varied. Some froze, some acted automatically, and others relied heavily on the presence of more experienced soldiers. Afterward, the psychological impact often remained. The realization that death was immediate and constant changed how soldiers approached everything that followed. The first encounter wasn't just a battle; it was a shift in perception, in which the abstract idea of war became a direct, personal experience.

187. Replacements: The Most Dangerous Day at the Front

New soldiers didn't usually arrive with their unit. Instead, they were sent forward as individual replacements, often at night, handed over to a squad they had never met. Veterans viewed them with a mixture of pity and distance. Newcomers were called "replacements," "fresh meat," or simply "new guys," and many weren't expected to last long. The first hours were often the most dangerous. Replacements didn't yet know the terrain, the routines, or the instincts that kept others alive. They might stand up at the wrong time, expose themselves, or misunderstand orders under fire. Veterans sometimes avoided learning their names immediately, knowing that many would be killed within days. This created a quiet divide within units. Survival wasn't only about skill but also about experience, and experience was measured in days. A soldier who lasted a week was already considered lucky. Those who survived longer became part of the group, but the constant arrival of replacements meant that units were always changing, always losing, and always rebuilding.

188. Desert Heat, Sand, and Thirst

In North Africa, soldiers fought in an environment that could be as dangerous as combat itself. The desert stretched across vast regions, including parts of the Sahara, where temperatures often reached around 110 degrees Fahrenheit (43 degrees Celsius) during the day and dropped close to freezing at night. These extreme shifts placed constant stress on the body. Soldiers suffered from heat exhaustion under the intense sun and from cold exposure after sunset, often without adequate shelter. Shade was rare, and even metal equipment could become too hot to touch. Prolonged exposure led to burns, dehydration, and fatigue, reducing combat effectiveness even before contact with the enemy. Water was the most critical resource. Supplies had to be transported over long distances, leading to frequent shortages. Rations could be as low as one pint (about half a liter) per day, which had to cover drinking, cooking, and basic hygiene. Washing was often impossible, leaving soldiers covered in dust and sweat. Dehydration became a constant threat, affecting concentration, strength, and decision-making. Food was also affected by the environment, which was often dry and salty, with sand frequently contaminating meals. In this setting, survival depended on endurance as much as training, as the desert itself constantly weakened those fighting within it.

189. Sand, Machinery, and Improvisation in the Desert War

Beyond heat and thirst, sand became a persistent enemy that affected nearly every aspect of warfare. Fine desert dust penetrated weapons, watches, radios, and vehicles, often causing equipment to fail. Rifles jammed easily, and tank engines suffered heavy damage as sand acted like an abrasive, wearing down moving parts. Maintenance became a daily necessity, with soldiers repeatedly cleaning weapons and machinery just to keep them operational. Goggles and scarves were used to protect eyes and lungs, particularly during sandstorms, which could reduce visibility to almost nothing and bring operations to a halt. With little natural cover, soldiers relied on vehicles or shallow dugouts for protection from both the sun and enemy observation. The open terrain made concealment difficult, making movement easily spotted and often dangerous. To cope with these harsh conditions, soldiers improvised. One example was the British "Benghazi Burner," a simple stove made from a biscuit tin filled with sand and petrol, used to heat water for tea. Tea became more than a drink; it was a routine that provided comfort and a sense of normality. In North Africa, survival required constant adaptation, as soldiers learned to manage not only the enemy but also the environment itself, which shaped how battles were fought and how long men could endure.

190. Frozen Fronts and the "White Death"

On the Eastern Front, the winter of 1941 brought some of the coldest temperatures recorded in decades, dropping to around minus forty degrees Fahrenheit (minus forty degrees Celsius). This period, often referred to as "General Winter," became a decisive factor in the fighting. The cold affected not only soldiers but also the technology on which modern armies depended. Synthetic oils used in engines and weapons froze solid, preventing tanks, trucks, and artillery from functioning. Machine guns and rifles could jam or fail completely, leaving soldiers unable to fire when needed. German crews often had to improvise simply to keep equipment operational. Fires were lit beneath vehicles to warm engines, and weapons were cleaned constantly in attempts to prevent freezing. Despite these efforts, many machines became unusable. The failure of equipment slowed movement, disrupted supply lines, and reduced the effectiveness of coordinated attacks. In a war that relied heavily on mechanization, the environment itself became a powerful opponent, limiting both mobility and firepower. The cold turned technology from an advantage into a liability, showing that even advanced military systems could be rendered ineffective by extreme conditions.

191. Survival, Frostbite, and the "White Death"

For soldiers, survival in the extreme cold depended on clothing, adaptation, and endurance. The difference in equipment between armies had serious consequences. Soviet troops were often issued valenki, thick felt boots that provided insulation and allowed circulation, helping prevent frostbite. German soldiers, however, wore tight leather jackboots with metal hobnails, which conducted cold and restricted blood flow. During the first winter alone, over 100,000 German troops suffered frostbite, many losing toes, fingers, or entire limbs. Soldiers improvised constantly to survive. Boots and uniforms were stuffed with newspaper, straw, or animal fur to add insulation. Even simple mistakes could be dangerous. Touching metal with bare skin could cause it to freeze instantly, tearing flesh away when pulled. The landscape itself created additional hazards. Snowstorms produced "whiteout" conditions, erasing visibility and making navigation nearly impossible. Units could become disoriented, leading to separation or ambush. The most feared threat was hypothermia, often called the "White Death." Exhausted soldiers could become numb and disoriented, experiencing a false sense of warmth before losing consciousness. In the absolute exhaustion of the front, thousands of men succumbed to a fatal lethargy, a deceptive feeling of warmth that precedes freezing, falling asleep in their foxholes and simply never waking up.

192. Jungle Warfare and the "Green Hell"

In the Pacific, soldiers encountered an environment so hostile that it became known as the "Green Hell." Unlike the open deserts of North Africa, the jungle was dense, enclosed, and constantly alive with moisture and sound. In places like Guadalcanal and New Guinea, humidity often reached ninety percent, with rainfall exceeding 200 inches (508 centimeters) per year. Rain wasn't an occasional event but a constant presence, soaking clothing, weapons, and supplies day after day. Nothing stayed dry. Uniforms clung to the body, boots remained wet, and equipment rusted quickly. Even after the rain stopped, the thick canopy of the jungle trapped moisture, preventing anything from fully drying. Visibility was extremely limited. Dense vegetation, vines, and thick undergrowth often reduced sightlines to less than ten feet (about three meters). Soldiers could move only slowly, cutting through foliage or following narrow paths. This created an atmosphere of constant tension.

The enemy could be just a few meters away, completely hidden by the jungle. Gunfire often erupted suddenly at close range, leaving little time to react. The noise of insects, birds, and the environment itself masked movement, making it difficult to detect approaching forces. Combat in the jungle was often confused and fragmented, and fought at extremely close distances. Movement through the jungle was exhausting. The ground was often muddy, uneven, and covered in thick vegetation. In some areas, soldiers had to push through kunai grass, which had sharp edges that cut exposed skin. Elsewhere, mud could reach knee or even thigh depth, making each step physically demanding. Carrying equipment under these conditions quickly led to exhaustion. Supply lines were difficult to maintain, meaning that food, ammunition, and medical supplies weren't always reliable. Units often operated in isolation, cut off from immediate support.

193. Disease, Survival, and Psychological Strain

The environment itself caused severe physical damage. Constant moisture led to conditions such as "jungle rot," a painful infection where the skin broke down into open sores due to prolonged exposure to wet conditions. Feet were particularly vulnerable. Soldiers' boots could rot within weeks, and skin that remained wet for long periods became soft, cracked, and easily infected. This condition, similar to trench foot, could disable soldiers even without combat injuries. Clothing wore out quickly, and replacement supplies weren't always available, forcing soldiers to endure deteriorating gear. Disease was one of the most significant threats. Mosquitoes thrived in the warm, wet conditions, spreading illnesses such as malaria and dengue fever. In some units, disease caused far more casualties than combat, sometimes five times as many. Soldiers were required to take Atabrine tablets to prevent malaria, but these caused side effects, including turning the skin a noticeable yellow color. Some soldiers avoided taking the medication due to these effects, increasing their risk of illness. Fever, weakness, and prolonged recovery times weakenedentire units. The psychological impact of jungle warfare was also significant. The constant noise, limited visibility, and ever-present threat of ambush created a sense of isolation and uncertainty. Soldiers could rarely see the larger battlefield and often had little understanding of their position relative to the enemy. The jungle removed the sense of distance that existed in other theaters of war. Combat was immediate, personal, and unpredictable.

194. Mountains, Mud, and the "Vertical War"

The Italian campaign quickly devolved into a grueling "Vertical War" as soldiers were forced to fight their way up the jagged spine of the Apennine Mountains. This geography provided a massive advantage to the German defenders, who occupied the "high ground," turning every mountain peak into a natural fortress. Allied troops, including Americans, British, Canadians, and Poles, had to haul heavy machine guns, mortars, and ammunition crates up sixty-degree slopes on their backs, often while under direct observation and fire from German snipers and artillery positioned thousands of feet above them. The misery of the terrain was multiplied by the weather, specifically the Italian version of "Rasputitsa," a relentless rainy season that transformed the volcanic soil into a thick, glue-like mud. This "mountain muck" was so deep that it swallowed Jeeps up to their axles and rendered tanks useless on the narrow, winding valley roads. Consequently, the high-tech Allied armies had to revert to older methods. Mules became the only reliable form of transport, carrying food, ammunition, and water up steep slopes and bringing wounded men back down. A single division might require over 1,000 mules just to remain supplied, showing how modern warfare could still depend on pre-industrial solutions in extreme terrain.

195. Exposure, Fortifications, and Attrition

During the brutal winter of 1944, the fighting reached its most stagnant and punishing phase. Because the rocky ground was too hard to dig into for traditional foxholes, soldiers were forced to live in sangars, dry-stone breastworks, or small "nests" built above ground from loose rocks. These offered limited protection against small-arms fire but provided almost no shelter from the environment. Men lived for weeks on exposed mountain peaks, enduring freezing rain, snow, and relentless winds that cut through clothing and made rest difficult. In this environment, progress was painfully slow. Military advances were no longer measured in miles but in individual ridges, hills, and ruined farmhouses. Each position often had a number, and capturing a single hill could cost hundreds of lives. Even after taking it, soldiers frequently found themselves facing another, higher position still held by the enemy. This constant uphill struggle turned the Italian campaign into a war of attrition that exhausted even experienced units. The landscape itself became a defensive weapon, demonstrating that terrain and weather could be as decisive as any army or technology.

196. Lice, Latrines, and the Spread of Disease

Life at the front exposed soldiers to constant health risks that weren't directly related to combat. Hygiene was difficult to maintain, especially in static positions where water was limited. Lice, small parasitic insects that live in clothing and bedding, spread rapidly among troops. They caused itching and skin irritation and, in some cases, transmitted diseases such as typhus. Soldiers often spent time picking lice from their uniforms or holding clothes over flames in an attempt to kill them. Sanitation was another major problem. Latrines were usually simple pits dug into the ground, often close to living areas. If not properly managed, they attracted insects and spread contamination. Combined with poor water quality, this led to outbreaks of illness, including dysentery, which caused severe dehydration and weakness. Medical care existed, but resources were limited, and treatment wasn't always immediate. These conditions reminded soldiers that danger didn't only come from enemy fire. Disease, discomfort, and poor hygiene were constant threats that affected entire units.

197. Artillery, Noise, and the Constant Threat from Above

One of the most defining features of the battlefield wasn't direct fighting but artillery fire. Large guns positioned far behind the front lines fired shells over long distances, meaning soldiers could be targeted without ever seeing the enemy. These shells produced explosions that caused both physical destruction and psychological strain. The sound of artillery was constant. Incoming shells could be heard as a distant whistle or sudden rush before impact, giving soldiers only seconds or no warning at all. Explosions threw dirt, metal fragments, and debris into the air, making even well-prepared positions unsafe. The unpredictability made it difficult to feel secure. A position that seemed safe one moment could be destroyed the next. Living under artillery fire created ongoing stress. Sleep was interrupted, communication was difficult, and movement became dangerous. Even when not actively under attack, the possibility of bombardment remained. Over time, this environment affected concentration and morale. Soldiers learned to recognize different sounds and react quickly, but the strain of constant exposure never fully disappeared. The battlefield wasn't only a place of action but also one of waiting, listening, and enduring.

198. Rumors, Misinformation, and the War of Stories

Most soldiers knew very little about the larger war. Information was limited, delayed, or deliberately controlled by high-level commanders. In this vacuum of facts, rumors, often called "latrine rumors" by the troops, spread with lightning speed and were frequently believed as gospel truth. Stories circulated constantly: that the war would end by Christmas, that reinforcements were arriving, or that the enemy was about to surrender. Conversely, dark rumors of secret weapons or massive defeats could shatter a unit's morale in hours. Soldiers relied on fragments to build their worldview: overheard conversations between officers, heavily censored letters from home, captured enemy newspapers they couldn't fully read, or "scuttlebutt" from passing transport units. These pieces were almost always incomplete or incorrect, but they offered a desperate sense of control in a situation where the truth was a luxury. One of the most famous examples of this "War of Stories" occurred during the Battle of the Bulge in 1944, involving "Operation Greif." Under the command of Otto Skorzeny, a small group of German soldiers dressed in captured American uniforms, driving American Jeeps, and speaking English, were sent behind U.S. lines to cause chaos. While their military impact was limited, the rumors they sparked were devastating. Word spread among American troops that thousands of German "spies" were everywhere, led by an elite team tasked with assassinating General Dwight D. Eisenhower. This single rumor paralyzed Allied movement for days. To catch the "impostors," American soldiers began setting up roadblocks and began "testing" each other with questions only a "real" American would know, such as "Who is Mickey Mouse's girlfriend?" or "What is the capital of Illinois?" Even high-ranking officers were detained; General Omar Bradley was famously held for a short time by his own men because he correctly identified the capital of Illinois as Springfield, but the guard mistakenly believed it was Chicago. These stories show that on the battlefield, a well-placed rumor could be just as disruptive as a direct artillery strike.

199. Wounds, Shock, and Immediate Survival

When a soldier was hit, survival depended on what happened in the first few minutes. Wounds varied widely, from small fragments to severe injuries caused by artillery, which was responsible for many of the most serious casualties. Soldiers were trained to carry basic first-aid kits, often including bandages and morphine syrettes, small pre-filled tubes used to inject pain relief. If a man was able, he was expected to treat himself or assist others nearby. The greatest immediate danger was often not the wound itself, but shock and blood loss. Shock could cause the body to shut down, even if the injury wasn't fatal. Fellow soldiers played a crucial role, applying pressure to wounds, offering reassurance, and trying to move the injured to safer positions. This was often done under fire, where helping someone could expose others to the same danger. Training emphasized speed and calm, but in reality, conditions were rarely controlled. Noise, fear, and confusion made even simple actions difficult. A wounded soldier's chances depended heavily on how quickly help arrived. In many cases, survival was determined not by the severity of the injury but by how long it took to reach medical care.

200. Fear, Fatigue, and the Limits of Endurance

Beyond physical danger, soldiers faced a constant mental strain that was often harder to measure but just as damaging. Fear wasn't limited to moments of combat. It existed before, during, and after engagements, shaped by uncertainty and the awareness that danger could come at any time. Even in quiet periods, soldiers remained alert, listening for distant sounds that might signal an attack. Fatigue made this pressure more difficult to manage. Sleep was often interrupted by noise, duty shifts, or the need to remain ready. Long periods without proper rest reduced concentration and slowed reactions, increasing the risk of mistakes. Hunger, cold, and illness added to this exhaustion. Over time, these conditions affected judgment and emotional stability. Some soldiers experienced what was then called "combat fatigue," where the mind became overwhelmed by stress. Symptoms could include shaking, withdrawal, confusion, or an inability to respond to orders. Armies developed systems to manage this, often removing affected soldiers from the front temporarily. However, not all cases were recognized or treated. For many, the pressure built gradually, showing that the battlefield tested not only the body but also the limits of human endurance.

201. Discipline, Punishment, and Control

Military discipline remained strict, even in combat zones. Soldiers were expected to follow orders immediately, maintain equipment, and remain at their posts regardless of danger. Failure to do so could result in punishment, ranging from loss of pay and duties to imprisonment or, in extreme cases, execution. Desertion (abandoning one's post) was one of the most serious offenses. Some armies carried out executions as a warning to others, particularly in the early years of the war. More commonly, punishment took the form of exhausting labor, confinement, or reassignment to dangerous duties. However, enforcement varied. Experienced officers often understood the limits of endurance and sometimes chose to overlook minor violations, knowing that survival depended on morale as much as strict obedience. In other cases, discipline was harshly enforced to maintain control amid chaotic conditions. For soldiers, discipline was both necessary and feared. It provided structure, but it also meant that the line between survival and punishment could be very thin.

202. Camaraderie, Routine, and Small Acts of Normal Life

Despite the harsh conditions, soldiers developed ways to cope with daily life at the front. One of the most important was camaraderie. Living, working, and facing danger together created strong bonds within small groups. Soldiers often relied on each other not only for support in combat but also for maintaining morale during quieter moments. Routine also played a key role. Cleaning equipment, preparing meals, standing guard, and maintaining positions provided structure in an otherwise unpredictable environment. Even simple tasks helped create a sense of control. Humor was another common response. Jokes, stories, and shared experiences allowed soldiers to release tension, even in difficult situations. These small elements, friendship and routine, helped soldiers manage the emotional demands of war. While they didn't remove the dangers, they provided moments of stability, allowing individuals to continue functioning in an environment where normal life had largely disappeared.

203. Nicknames, Identity, and Losing the Individual

As soldiers settled into units, individual identity often shifted. Nicknames replaced formal names, based on personality, appearance, or origin. These names were used more frequently than official ones, especially within small groups. Uniforms, routines, and shared experiences created a sense of collective identity. Soldiers became part of a unit first, individuals second. Personal differences were less important than reliability and cooperation. Over time, the war could blur individuality. Soldiers were known by their role, their position, or their function within the group. This helped units operate efficiently, but it also changed how individuals saw themselves. Identity became tied to survival and belonging. Being part of the group was essential, both practically and emotionally.

204. Letters, Censorship, and the Lifeline to Home

For most soldiers, letters were the primary connection to life beyond the battlefield. Postal systems were organized on a massive scale to move mail between the front and home, often across continents and active war zones. In many armies, soldiers were encouraged to write regularly, and mail was delivered whenever conditions allowed. Some units received letters weekly, while others, especially in remote or active combat zones, might wait weeks or even months. Letters were both personal and controlled. Military authorities censored outgoing and incoming mail to prevent sensitive information from being revealed. Soldiers weren't allowed to mention locations, movements, or details that could compromise security. As a result, many letters focused on everyday topics, health, weather, and small routines, while avoiding the realities of combat. Families at home often received a version of the war that was quieter and less dangerous than what soldiers actually experienced. Writing letters served an important emotional purpose. It allowed soldiers to maintain a sense of identity beyond their role in the war. Receiving a letter could improve morale, while long periods without news could create anxiety and isolation. Some soldiers carried letters with them, reading them repeatedly during quiet moments. In a setting where uncertainty was constant, communication with home became one of the few stable and meaningful connections they could rely on.

205. Alcohol, Cigarettes, and Small Escapes

In a life defined by danger, discomfort, and uncertainty, soldiers relied on small habits to cope. Among the most common were alcohol and cigarettes. These weren't luxuries in the traditional sense; they were part of daily life, used to manage stress, fatigue, and fear. Cigarettes were especially widespread. Many armies issued them as part of regular rations, alongside food and ammunition. Soldiers smoked during rest periods, after meals, and sometimes even in combat zones when conditions allowed. Lighting a cigarette could mark a moment of calm, however brief, or provide something to do while waiting. It also became a form of social exchange. Cigarettes were traded, shared, and used to build connections between soldiers. For some, smoking became a constant habit, a way to steady nerves or pass time in an environment where little was under their control. Alcohol served a different purpose. When available, it was often issued in controlled amounts, such as rum for British troops or vodka for Soviet soldiers. These rations were intended to boost morale, provide warmth in cold conditions, or help soldiers relax after long periods of tension. In some cases, alcohol was consumed before or after combat, dulling fear or offering temporary relief from the realities of the battlefield. Access to alcohol varied. In rear areas or occupied regions, soldiers sometimes obtained additional supplies through trade or requisition. However, strict discipline was usually enforced, and excessive drinking was often punished, especially if it affected performance. Despite this, alcohol remained a common part of military life, particularly during moments away from direct combat. Both cigarettes and alcohol functioned as forms of escape.

206. Death, Burial, and Living Among the Fallen

Death was a constant presence on the battlefield, and soldiers were often exposed to it in ways that were difficult to avoid. Bodies could remain in the open for extended periods, especially in areas of heavy fighting where movement was dangerous. This created a situation where soldiers had to continue their duties while surrounded by the remains of those who had fallen. Whenever possible, units attempted to bury the dead. These burials were often simple and carried out quickly, using shallow graves marked with temporary signs such as helmets, rifles, or wooden crosses. In some cases, identification tags were collected to record who had died, while personal belongings were gathered for sending home. However, conditions didn't always allow for proper burial, and many soldiers remained where they had fallen until later recovery. Living in proximity to death affected morale and mental state. It served as a constant reminder of risk and loss, reinforcing the reality of the situation. Soldiers developed ways to cope, sometimes through routine, silence, or emotional distance. The presence of death wasn't an isolated event but an ongoing part of daily life at the front.

207. Missing, Prisoners, and the Uncertainty of Fate

Not all soldiers who disappeared in battle were confirmed dead. Many were listed as missing, leaving families and units uncertain about their fate. In the confusion of combat, it was often difficult to determine what had happened. A soldier might be separated from their unit, captured, or killed without immediate confirmation. This uncertainty could last for months or years. Capture brought a different set of challenges. Prisoners of war were removed from the battlefield, but their conditions depended on where they were held and how they were treated. Some camps provided basic shelter, food, and medical care, while others were marked by shortages and harsh conditions. Prisoners often faced hunger, illness, and long periods of inactivity, along with uncertainty about when or if they would be released. For those who remained at the front, the knowledge that capture or disappearance was possible added another layer of tension. War didn't always provide clear outcomes. Survival, death, or captivity could all occur without warning, leaving both soldiers and their families dealing with uncertainty long after the fighting had moved on.

208. POW Cages, Stalags, and the Slow Violence of Captivity

Between 1940 and 1945, many British and Commonwealth soldiers became prisoners during major defeats in France, Greece/Crete, and North Africa, often after chaotic surrenders, encirclements, or being cut off from evacuation routes. Many described capture as a shock: weapons taken, identity reduced to a number, then forced marches or transport in crowded trains toward camps across German-occupied Europe. Camps were commonly divided into Stalags (for enlisted men) and Oflags (for officers). Under the 1929 Geneva Convention, enlisted prisoners could be required to work (often farm or industrial labor), while officers were generally not compelled to do so, though reality varied by location and conditions. Even when treatment was "lawful" by wartime standards, hunger, boredom, lice, and exhaustion were constant. Escapes happened, but many prisoners were simply too weak, too watched, or too far from safe borders to risk it, so survival became a daily discipline of routine, makeshift education, and waiting.

209. Rotation, Leave, and Moments Away from the Front

Despite the constant demands of war, most armies recognized that soldiers couldn't remain on the front line indefinitely. Over time, systems developed to rotate units out of combat for short periods of rest. These breaks could take place in rear areas, away from immediate danger, where soldiers were given time to recover physically and mentally. Conditions in these areas varied. Some provided basic comforts such as hot food, medical care, and the opportunity to sleep without interruption. Others were little more than safer zones, still exposed to occasional danger. Even limited rest could make a significant difference, allowing soldiers to clean their equipment, wash, and regain strength. Leave, when granted, allowed soldiers to return home for a brief period. This created a sharp contrast between the front and civilian life. Some found comfort in familiar surroundings, while others struggled to adjust, knowing they would soon return to combat. The experience could feel temporary and distant from the realities of war. These breaks didn't remove the pressures of conflict, but they provided moments of relief. They allowed soldiers to continue functioning over long periods, offering a brief return to normal life before facing the front again.

210. The End of War and the Return to Civilian Life

When the war ended in 1945, the experience of soldiers didn't simply stop. For many, the transition back to civilian life was gradual and uncertain. Demobilization (the process of releasing soldiers from service) took time, and not all units returned home immediately. Some remained in occupied territories, while others waited months for transport to become available. Returning home brought its own challenges. Soldiers had spent years in structured, high-pressure environments, and adjusting to civilian life required a different set of skills. Routines that had once defined daily life were gone, and the sense of purpose tied to military service was often difficult to replace. Physical injuries were visible, but psychological effects were less obvious. Some veterans struggled with memories of combat, loss, and prolonged stress. Others found it difficult to communicate their experiences to those who had not been at the front. At the same time, there was a sense of relief that the conflict had ended. Families were reunited, and societies began rebuilding. The end of the war marked a transition not just for nations but also for individuals who had lived through it. The experience of being a soldier didn't disappear with peace. It remained part of their lives long after the fighting had stopped.

SIX

Medical Survival and Innovation

World War II forced rapid advancements in medicine as doctors and scientists worked to treat injuries on a scale never before encountered. New techniques, equipment, and procedures were developed in response to the urgent need to save lives, often under extremely difficult conditions. This chapter explores the medical challenges of the war, from battlefield treatment and evacuation systems to the development of new drugs and surgical methods. It highlights how necessity drove innovation, leading to breakthroughs that would influence medicine long after the war had ended.

211. First Aid, Field Surgery, and the Race Against Time

At the beginning of the war, survival for a wounded soldier depended less on advanced medicine and more on speed and organization. Most armies relied on systems developed during World War I, where the goal was to stabilize a soldier quickly and move him away from the front as fast as possible. Every soldier carried a basic field dressing and, in some cases, morphine to control pain and bleeding immediately after injury. The first stage of care usually took place at a regimental aid post, often located just behind the front line. These were small, makeshift stations, sometimes in tents, barns, or damaged buildings, where medics worked under constant pressure. Conditions were rarely sterile. Mud, blood, and debris were common, and supplies were limited. Doctors focused on immediate survival: stopping bleeding, preventing shock, and preparing the wounded for evacuation. From there, soldiers were moved further back to field dressing stations and field hospitals, where more complex procedures could be performed. However, getting a wounded soldier to these locations was often dangerous and slow. Stretcher-bearers had to carry men across open ground, sometimes under fire, or wait for vehicles that might not arrive quickly. Even in these difficult conditions, the system saved many lives. What mattered most was time. The faster a wounded soldier reached medical care, the greater his chances of survival, making speed the most important factor in early wartime medicine.

212. Blood Transfusions and the Creation of Wartime Blood Banks

One of the most important medical advances during the early years of the war was the development of large-scale blood transfusion systems. Severe blood loss was one of the leading causes of death on the battlefield, and earlier wars had shown that replacing lost blood could dramatically improve survival. During World War II, this idea was expanded into organized national systems. In Britain, doctors such as Janet Vaughan helped establish one of the first large-scale blood banks. Blood was collected from civilian donors, carefully stored, and transported to military hospitals. By 1940, refrigerated blood supplies were being sent to treat casualties during air raids and on overseas fronts. This allowed wounded soldiers to receive transfusions even far from major hospitals. The United States developed similar systems, with a particular focus on blood plasma. Plasma, the liquid component of blood, could be dried, stored for long periods, and reconstituted when needed. Unlike whole blood, it didn't require strict matching of blood types, making it easier to use in emergency situations. This made plasma especially valuable in forward medical units, where time and conditions were critical. The introduction of transfusions significantly improved battlefield survival rates. Soldiers who might previously have died from shock could now be stabilized long enough to reach surgery. However, challenges remained. Blood had to be kept at controlled temperatures, supplies could be limited, and mishandling could be dangerous. Despite these risks, the development of blood banks marked a major turning point.

213. The Arrival of Penicillin and the Fight Against Infection

At the beginning of the war, infection was often more dangerous than the original wound. Even a minor injury could become fatal if bacteria entered the body. Dirt, fabric, and metal fragments carried into wounds created ideal conditions for infection, and without effective antibiotics, doctors relied on older methods such as cleaning, draining, and applying antiseptics. Despite these efforts, diseases like gangrene (tissue death) and sepsis (blood poisoning) were common, and amputation was often the only way to save a life. The introduction of penicillin changed this reality. First discovered in 1928, penicillin wasn't widely available until the early 1940s, when scientists in Britain and the United States developed methods to produce it on a large scale. By 1943, it began reaching frontline medical units, and by 1944, it was widely used by Allied forces. Penicillin works by killing bacteria that cause infections, allowing wounds to heal more effectively. For the first time, doctors could treat infections directly rather than just managing their symptoms. This reduced the need for amputations and dramatically improved survival rates, particularly for soldiers with severe injuries. However, early supplies were limited. Doctors often had to decide which patients would receive the drug, prioritizing those most likely to survive. In some cases, penicillin was even extracted from patients' urine and reused, reflecting how valuable it was. The widespread use of penicillin marked a major shift in wartime medicine.

214. Sulfa Drugs, Infection Control, and the "First Line of Defense"

Before penicillin became widely available, the primary defense against infection came from sulfa drugs, a group of synthetic antibiotics developed in the 1930s. These drugs were among the first effective treatments against bacterial infections and were issued to soldiers as part of their personal medical kits. Each soldier often carried a small packet of sulfa powder, intended to be applied directly to wounds as soon as possible. If a soldier was injured, he or a nearby comrade would sprinkle the powder onto the wound before applying a bandage. This immediate treatment could slow the growth of bacteria, reducing the risk of infection before the wounded soldier reached a medic. Medics also used sulfa drugs in larger quantities at aid stations, combining them with cleaning and dressing wounds. While not as powerful as penicillin, sulfa drugs were widely available and easy to use, making them essential during the early and middle years of the war. In addition to medication, infection control depended heavily on basic practices. Wounds were cleaned as thoroughly as possible, damaged tissue was removed, and dressings were changed regularly. These procedures were often performed in difficult conditions, sometimes in tents or improvised shelters close to the front. Despite these efforts, infection remained a constant threat, especially in environments like jungles or muddy battlefields where bacteria thrived. The combination of sulfa drugs, improved surgical techniques, and later penicillin gradually reduced death rates, but the risk never fully disappeared.

215. Venereal Disease, Discipline, and the Hidden Strain on Armies

Beyond wounds and infection, armies faced another persistent medical problem: venereal disease (V.D.), particularly gonorrhea and syphilis. Soldiers stationed far from home, often dealing with loneliness, boredom, and long periods of inactivity, frequently sought companionship, thereby spreading infection across many theaters of war. During World War I, V.D. had incapacitated tens of thousands of soldiers daily, and although rates were significantly reduced by World War II, it remained a serious issue. By 1944, hundreds of servicemen were still removed from duty each day due to infection. Military authorities responded with a combination of medical treatment, education, and discipline. Soldiers received pamphlets, lectures, and warning posters emphasizing sexual hygiene and the risks of infection. Condoms and chemical prophylaxis kits were distributed, sometimes free of charge, and special "prophylactic stations" were established where soldiers could receive immediate treatment after exposure. Advances in medicine, particularly sulfa drugs and penicillin, dramatically reduced recovery time. A case of gonorrhea that once required weeks of hospitalization could be treated in days. However, the issue wasn't only medical but also disciplinary. In some units, infection could result in punishment, including loss of rank or restricted duties. This created tension between prevention, personal behavior, and military control. Venereal disease became a quiet but constant challenge, affecting manpower, morale, and the daily functioning of armies far from home.

216. Triage and the Hard Decisions of Who Lives

As the number of wounded increased, especially during large-scale offensives, medical teams faced a critical problem: there were often more injured soldiers than they could treat at once. This led to the widespread use of triage, a system that prioritized patients based on their chances of survival and the urgency of their injuries. At regimental aid posts and field hospitals, wounded soldiers were quickly assessed and placed into categories. Those with minor injuries who could return to duty quickly were treated first, as they could be sent back to the front. Soldiers with serious but survivable wounds were also prioritized, as timely treatment could save their lives. Those who were too severely wounded, with little chance of survival, were often given only basic care or pain relief. This system was practical, but it forced doctors and medics to make extremely difficult decisions. In some cases, they had to pass over severely wounded men who were still conscious, focusing instead on those who could be saved with limited resources. These decisions were made quickly, often under pressure, with little time for reflection. Triage changed how medical care functioned on the battlefield. It was no longer just about treating each individual; it was about managing large numbers of casualties and using resources where they could have the greatest impact. While it saved many lives, it also left some behind, not because they were unimportant, but because they couldn't be saved in time.

217. Surgery Without Time: Amputations, Exhaustion, and Battlefield Reality

In large battles, especially during the early and middle years of the war, medical systems were often overwhelmed. Field hospitals received waves of wounded soldiers faster than they could be treated. In these conditions, surgery became a continuous process rather than a controlled procedure. Surgeons worked long hours, sometimes operating for twelve to twenty-four hours without rest, moving from one patient to the next with little pause. The focus was speed and survival, not precision. Sterile conditions were difficult to maintain. Operations were often performed in tents, damaged buildings, or hastily prepared rooms close to the front. Lighting could be poor, especially at night or during blackout conditions, forcing surgeons to work under dim lighting. Supplies were limited, and anesthesia, when available, was sometimes reduced or delayed due to shortages or other urgent needs. In extreme situations, procedures had to begin before full preparation was possible. Amputation was one of the most common emergency operations. Severe limb injuries caused by artillery or crushing wounds left little choice. Removing a limb quickly could prevent infection or death from blood loss. These decisions were made in minutes. The scale of casualties meant that surgeons couldn't treat every injury in detail. They worked to keep as many men alive as possible, often under conditions of noise, exhaustion, and constant pressure. Survival depended not only on skill but also on endurance.

218. Medics Under Fire and the Role of Frontline Care

The first person to treat a wounded soldier was often not a doctor but a combat medic. These individuals operated on the front lines, moving through active combat zones to reach the injured. Medics worked without weapons in many armies, marked by symbols such as the Red Cross to indicate their non-combat role. Despite this, they were frequently exposed to the same dangers as infantry soldiers, including gunfire, artillery, and explosions. Reaching a wounded soldier could mean crawling across open ground or entering areas still under enemy fire. Their tasks were urgent and practical. They stopped bleeding, treated shock, administered pain relief, and prepared soldiers for evacuation. In many cases, the actions taken in these first few minutes determined whether a soldier would survive. Medics also had to decide when it was safe to move the wounded, balancing the risk of further injury against the danger of leaving them in place. The psychological pressure on medics was intense. They worked in proximity to severe injuries, often treating multiple casualties at once, while knowing that they couldn't save everyone. Many were recognized for acts of bravery, receiving medals for rescuing wounded soldiers under fire. Frontline medical care became a critical part of survival. It connected the battlefield to the larger medical system, ensuring that wounded soldiers had a chance to reach more advanced treatment further from the front.

219. Nurses in Field Hospitals: Care, Endurance, and Emotional Strain

Behind the front lines, nurses played a central role in caring for the wounded, often working in field hospitals and casualty clearing stations. These facilities received soldiers directly from evacuation routes, meaning nurses encountered injuries at their most severe. They assisted in surgery, changed dressings, managed infections, and monitored patients recovering from major trauma. Conditions were demanding. Hospitals were often overcrowded, especially during major offensives, with large numbers of wounded arriving within short periods. Nurses worked long shifts, sometimes for days at a time, with little rest, moving continuously between patients. Their role extended beyond medical care. Nurses provided reassurance, comfort, and human connection in a setting where many soldiers were far from home and facing pain or death. They wrote letters for the wounded, helped identify the dead, and supported men struggling with fear or shock. The emotional toll was significant. Nurses were exposed daily to severe injuries and loss, often forming brief but intense connections with patients who didn't survive. Despite these conditions, their work was essential to recovery. They maintained the continuity of care between surgery and healing, ensuring that wounded soldiers received ongoing attention in an environment where survival depended on both medical skill and constant support.

220. Jeeps, Ambulances, and the Race Against Time

Once a soldier received initial treatment at the front, the next step was evacuation, and speed became critical. The faster a wounded man could reach a surgical unit, the greater his chances of survival. This led to the widespread use of motorized evacuation systems, especially ambulances and jeeps adapted for carrying casualties. In earlier wars, wounded soldiers were often transported by horse or on foot. In World War II, motor vehicles became the backbone of evacuation. Jeeps were modified with stretcher racks, allowing two to three wounded men to be transported at once, even across rough terrain. Larger ambulances could carry more patients, but they required usable roads, which were often damaged or under fire. The journey itself was dangerous. Roads could be targeted by artillery or aircraft, and vehicles sometimes had to travel at night without headlights to avoid detection. In muddy or mountainous terrain, vehicles could become stuck, forcing stretcher-bearers to carry the wounded on foot over long distances. Time was everything. Medical teams aimed to move casualties from the front line to surgical care within hours. Delays increased the risk of infection, shock, and death. As a result, evacuation routes were planned carefully, and drivers often worked continuously, moving back and forth between the front and rear areas. The use of motorized transport transformed battlefield medicine. It allowed wounded soldiers to reach advanced care much faster than before, significantly improving survival rates, especially during large-scale operations.

221. Air Evacuation and the First Use of Helicopters

As the war progressed, a new method of evacuation emerged: air transport. Fixed-wing aircraft were increasingly used to move wounded soldiers from forward airstrips to hospitals further behind the lines. These flights were faster than ground transport and could bypass damaged roads or difficult terrain. Planes were often fitted with stretchers, allowing multiple patients to be transported at once. Medical personnel accompanied the wounded, providing care during the flight. Although conditions were basic, air evacuation reduced travel time from days to hours, greatly increasing survival rates for seriously injured soldiers. Near the end of the war, an even more experimental development appeared: the helicopter. Early models, such as the *Sikorsky R-4*, were used in limited numbers, particularly in the Pacific theater. These aircraft could land in areas inaccessible to planes or vehicles, including jungle clearings and mountainous terrain. Helicopters were slow and could carry only one or two patients at a time, but they demonstrated a new possibility: direct evacuation from the battlefield. In some cases, wounded soldiers were lifted out of areas that would have been impossible to reach by ground. Although still rare, these early helicopter evacuations marked the beginning of a major change in military medicine. They showed that rapid, direct extraction from combat zones was possible, a concept that would become standard in later conflicts.

222. Flight Nurses and Air Evacuation: Care in Transit

As air evacuation expanded, a new role emerged: the flight nurse. These nurses were trained to care for wounded soldiers during transport in aircraft, where conditions were far from stable. Planes often flew at low altitudes, in cold, noisy environments, with limited space and equipment. Wounded men were secured on stretchers, sometimes stacked in tiers, with little room for movement. Flight nurses monitored vital signs, administered medication, managed bleeding, and provided oxygen when available. They worked in difficult conditions, where turbulence, noise, and limited lighting made even simple tasks challenging. Communication was often reduced to gestures due to the sound of engines. Flights could last several hours, and patients were often in critical condition. Nurses had to respond quickly to changes, stabilizing soldiers who might deteriorate during transport. The goal was to keep them alive long enough to reach fully equipped hospitals further from the front. Air evacuation significantly reduced travel time, and the presence of trained medical staff during flights improved survival rates. For many soldiers, these flights marked the transition from immediate danger to recovery. Flight nurses became a vital link in the chain of care, ensuring that treatment continued even in transit, under conditions that required both medical skill and adaptability.

223. Burn Injuries, Aircrew Survival, and the "Guinea Pig Club"

One of the most severe injuries of the war came from burns, particularly among airmen. Pilots and bomber crews faced extreme risks: when aircraft were hit, fuel ignited instantly, turning cockpits into enclosed fires. Those who survived often suffered extensive burns to the face, hands, and upper body, injuries that were both life-threatening and permanently disfiguring. Early in the war, survival rates for severe burns were very low. Infection, shock, and fluid loss often led to death within days. Treatment was painful and limited, involving basic dressings and morphine for pain. Many doctors initially believed that patients with large-area burns couldn't survive. This changed through the work of surgeons such as Archibald McIndoe, working with the Royal Air Force. At Queen Victoria Hospital in England,

McIndoe developed new methods of treatment, including improved skin graft techniques and better management of infection and fluid loss. He also emphasized psychological recovery, recognizing that disfigurement affected identity as much as the body. Patients under his care formed a unique social group known as the "Guinea Pig Club," named after the experimental nature of their treatments. Members supported each other through long recoveries, often undergoing dozens of operations. They also engaged with local communities, helping reduce stigma around disfigurement. These advances significantly improved survival rates. Burn victims who would have died earlier in the war were now able to live, though often with lasting physical and emotional scars.

224. Plastic Surgery, Reconstruction, and Rebuilding Faces

Beyond survival, one of the greatest medical challenges of the war was reconstruction, helping soldiers live with injuries that changed their appearance and function. Explosions, shrapnel, and burns often caused severe damage to the face, including the loss of noses, jaws, or eyes. Plastic surgery, still a developing field, advanced rapidly during the war. Surgeons developed techniques to rebuild damaged areas using skin grafts and "flap" procedures, where skin and tissue were moved from one part of the body to another while maintaining a blood supply. These operations were often performed in stages, requiring multiple surgeries over months or years. For many patients, recovery wasn't just physical. Facial injuries affected speech, eating, and social interaction. Some soldiers were reluctant to return home, fearing how they would be perceived. Hospitals began to address these concerns, encouraging patients to socialize and rebuild confidence alongside physical treatment. Artificial replacements, or prosthetics, were also developed for missing features such as eyes, noses, or parts of the jaw. While not perfect, these helped restore some appearance and function. Dental reconstruction became particularly important, allowing soldiers to eat and speak more normally. These medical efforts transformed survival into long-term recovery. Soldiers who might previously have lived isolated lives were given the chance to reintegrate into society. The techniques developed during this period became the basis for modern reconstructive and cosmetic surgery, showing that medicine wasn't only about saving lives but also about restoring them.

225. Combat Fatigue" and the Recognition of Psychological Collapse

As the war intensified, armies began to face a problem they couldn't ignore: soldiers who were physically unharmed but no longer able to fight. Early in the war, these men were often labeled as cowards or accused of lacking discipline. Terms like "shell shock" from World War I were still used, but understanding remained limited. By 1941–1942, especially on the Eastern Front, in North Africa, and later in Italy and France, the scale of psychological breakdown became impossible to dismiss. Soldiers exposed to constant artillery fire, exhaustion, and fear began to show clear symptoms: shaking, confusion, inability to speak, paralysis without injury, or complete withdrawal. Some wandered aimlessly; others couldn't follow orders or even recognize their surroundings. This condition became known as "combat fatigue" or "battle exhaustion." Studies showed that even well-trained soldiers had limits. In some units, it was estimated that up to one in four soldiers would experience some form of psychological breakdown if exposed to combat long enough. Armies began to change their approach. Rather than punishing these soldiers, the medical staff was instructed to treat them as casualties. The key principle became "PIE" treatment: Proximity (treat near the front), Immediacy (treat quickly), and Expectation (expect recovery). Soldiers were given rest, food, and reassurance, often just for a few days, before being returned to duty. This approach had mixed results, but it marked a major shift. War was no longer seen as a test of will alone. It revealed that the human mind, like the body, could be pushed beyond its limits.

226. Psychiatric Units, Forward Treatment, and the Strain of Endurance

By the later years of the war, psychiatric care became more organized and structured. Dedicated forward psychiatric units were established close to the front lines, designed to treat soldiers before their condition worsened. The idea was simple: remove the soldier briefly from combat, provide rest, food, and calm, and then return him to his unit as quickly as possible. These centers were deliberately kept close to the battlefield so that soldiers didn't feel permanently removed from their role. Doctors believed that sending men too far to the rear made them less likely to return to duty. Treatment focused on simplicity. Soldiers were encouraged to sleep, eat, and talk about their experiences. In some cases, mild sedatives were used. The emphasis wasn't on deep therapy but on restoring basic functioning. Despite these efforts, the strain of continuous warfare remained overwhelming. Campaigns like Normandy, the Eastern Front, and the Pacific involved months of sustained combat with little relief. Soldiers rotated in and out of the line, but the cumulative effect of fear, loss, and exhaustion was constant. Some soldiers recovered and returned to their units. Others were evacuated further back and didn't return to combat. The war showed that psychological injury wasn't rare or exceptional; it was a common consequence of prolonged exposure to violence. These experiences influenced postwar medicine, contributing to later understanding of conditions such as post-traumatic stress disorder (PTSD).

SEVEN

Animals in War

Animals played a significant and often overlooked role in World War II. They were used for transport, communication, detection, and even direct participation in military operations. From horses and dogs to pigeons and dolphins, animals became part of the war effort in ways that were both practical and, at times, unexpected. This chapter examines the contributions of animals in the conflict, highlighting their roles on the battlefield and behind the lines. It also considers the risks they faced and the reliance that human forces placed on them during critical moments. It was a war in which not only humans but also animals were drawn into the demands and dangers of global conflict.

227. Horses in a "Modern" War

At the beginning of World War II, despite the presence of tanks and motor vehicles, horses remained essential to military operations. Germany alone relied on over 600,000 horses during the invasion of Poland in 1939, and by 1941, this number would grow to more than one million. The Wehrmacht (German Defense Force) was often perceived as fully mechanized, but in reality, much of its supply system depended on horse-drawn transport. Horses were used to pull artillery, wagons, and supply carts, especially in areas where roads were poor or damaged. In Eastern Europe, where infrastructure was limited, motor vehicles frequently broke down or became stuck in mud. Horses, by contrast, could move across rough terrain and required no fuel, making them more reliable in certain conditions. However, their use came at a high cost. Horses were vulnerable to exhaustion, extreme weather, and enemy fire. They required food and water, which placed additional strain on supply systems. During harsh winters or long campaigns, many died from overwork or starvation. In some cases, they were slaughtered to feed troops when supplies ran low. Although often overlooked, horses remained a crucial part of early war logistics. Their presence highlighted the contrast between modern weapons and traditional methods, showing that even in a mechanized war, older forms of transport still played a vital role.

228. Carrier Pigeons and the Lifeline of Communication

Before secure radio communication became widespread, carrier pigeons played a critical role in military operations. These birds were used by many countries, including Britain, Germany, and the United States, to carry messages across enemy lines. Their ability to return to their home lofts over long distances made them a reliable form of communication, especially when other systems failed. Pigeons were often used in situations where radio signals could be intercepted or jammed. A small message was placed in a capsule attached to the bird's leg, and the pigeon was released. It would then fly back to its base, sometimes covering distances of over 100 miles (160 kilometers). Because they flew at high speeds and were difficult to track, pigeons were less vulnerable to interception than human messengers. Their use was particularly important for isolated units. Soldiers cut off behind enemy lines could send information about their position, request assistance, or report enemy movements. In some cases, pigeons helped coordinate rescue operations or artillery support. However, the role was dangerous. Pigeons were often targeted by enemy forces, and many were lost during missions. Despite this, thousands were successfully delivered. Some birds became well-known for their service. One notable example from World War II was a pigeon named Winkie, who was awarded the Dickin Medal for her service. In February 1942, a damaged Royal Air Force bomber crashed into the North Sea during a mission. The crew released Winkie in the hope that she would return to her home loft and alert authorities. Although she carried no written message, her arrival time allowed officials to estimate the aircraft's location. A rescue mission was launched, and the crew was found shortly afterward. Winkie's flight demonstrated how even in an age of advancing technology, simple and natural methods of communication could still be vital to survival.

229. War Dogs as Messengers, Guards, and Lifesavers

Dogs were used extensively by nearly every army during the war, trained for a wide range of roles that combined instinct, intelligence, and loyalty. Germany, the Soviet Union, Britain, and the United States all developed specialized dog units, with tens of thousands of animals serving alongside soldiers. One of the most important roles was message carrying. In situations where radio communication was unreliable or dangerous, dogs could be sent between positions with written messages. Unlike human runners, they were smaller, faster, and less visible, making them harder to target. They could navigate terrain under fire, moving through trenches, forests, or ruined buildings. Dogs were also used as guard animals, particularly around camps, supply depots, and prisoner enclosures. Their hearing and sense of smell made them highly effective at detecting intruders, often alerting soldiers before any human could notice movement. In occupied territories, guard dogs were sometimes used in patrols, reinforcing control over civilian populations. Perhaps most valued were rescue dogs, especially on the Eastern Front and in areas of heavy fighting. These dogs were trained to search for wounded soldiers on the battlefield. Using their sense of smell, they could locate men buried under debris or lying unconscious in difficult terrain. Some carried small medical packs, allowing wounded soldiers to treat themselves, while others were trained to return to handlers and signal when they had found someone. For many soldiers, these animals were more than tools. They became companions in an environment defined by danger and uncertainty. A trained dog could mean the difference between life and death, whether by delivering a message, providing a warning, or finding a wounded man who might otherwise have been left behind.

230. Anti-Tank Dogs and the Brutal Experiments of War

One of the most controversial uses of animals during the war occurred in the Soviet Union, where dogs were trained for anti-tank missions. Faced with the rapid advance of German armored units during Operation Barbarossa in 1941, Soviet forces developed a desperate strategy to counter tanks. Dogs were trained to carry explosives on their backs and run underneath enemy tanks. The idea was that the explosive charge would detonate on contact, destroying the vehicle. Training often involved conditioning the dogs to associate tanks with food, encouraging them to run toward them during battle. In practice, the system proved deeply flawed. Dogs trained with Soviet diesel-powered tanks sometimes became confused when confronted with German tanks, which used different engines and smells. In some cases, they ran back toward the Soviet lines, creating danger for their own troops. Others panicked under fire or failed to reach their targets. Despite these problems, the program was used in combat, particularly in 1941 and 1942. Some tanks were reportedly destroyed, but the overall effectiveness was limited. The approach also raised serious ethical concerns, as it involved the deliberate sacrifice of animals in dangerous and often chaotic conditions. The use of anti-tank dogs reflected the extreme pressures of the Eastern Front. As losses mounted and resources were stretched, military planners turned to unconventional methods, even those that were unreliable or controversial. It showed how war could push both human and animal lives into roles shaped by urgency, desperation, and survival.

231. Mine Detection Dogs and the Hidden Danger Beneath the Ground

As the war progressed, landmines became one of the most persistent and deadly threats on the battlefield. Millions were laid across Europe, North Africa, and Asia, often hidden beneath soil, sand, or vegetation. These devices didn't distinguish between soldiers and civilians, and long after battles ended, they continued to kill and injure anyone who stepped on them. To counter this, armies increasingly relied on trained dogs to detect explosives. Dogs were trained to identify the scent of explosives such as TNT, even when buried underground. Handlers would guide them slowly across suspected areas, watching for specific behaviors, such as stopping, sitting, or pawing the ground, that indicated a possible mine. This method allowed soldiers to clear paths more safely than manual probing alone, which required individuals to search inch by inch with metal rods, often at great personal risk. Mine detection dogs were used by both Allied and Axis forces, but became especially important during and after major offensives, when large areas needed to be secured quickly. In Italy, France, and later Germany, they helped clear roads, fields, and abandoned defensive lines. Their work didn't end with combat; after the war, dogs continued to assist in clearing mines, allowing civilians to return to farmland and rebuild communities. Despite their effectiveness, the work was dangerous. A single mistake could be fatal. Many dogs were injured or killed during operations, but their ability to detect hidden threats saved countless human lives. Their role highlighted how war extended beyond visible danger, where survival often depended on finding what couldn't be seen.

232. Mascots, Companions, and the Emotional Survival of Soldiers

Beyond their official roles, animals became an important part of soldiers' emotional lives. Units often adopted mascots, which could include dogs, cats, goats, birds, or even more unusual animals such as monkeys or bears. These animals weren't trained for combat; they served a different purpose: providing comfort, familiarity, and a sense of normalcy in an environment dominated by stress and uncertainty. Mascots were often found locally or brought in from other areas and quickly became part of the unit. Soldiers named them, fed them, and cared for them collectively. In many cases, these animals moved with the unit, traveling through different fronts and becoming symbols of shared experience. Some mascots were even given unofficial ranks or uniforms, reflecting their integration into military culture. Animals also played a role in daily routines. A dog greeting soldiers returning from patrol, a cat in a trench, or a bird in a cage could provide small moments of calm. These interactions helped reduce stress and offered a distraction from constant danger. For soldiers far from home, animals could serve as a reminder of ordinary life, something familiar in a situation that was otherwise unpredictable. The loss of a mascot could affect morale significantly. Just as soldiers formed bonds with each other, they formed attachments to these animals. Their presence showed that survival wasn't only physical but also emotional. In a war defined by destruction, these small relationships provided moments of connection, helping soldiers endure the psychological strain of prolonged conflict.

233. Unusual Animal Roles and the Story of Wojtek the Bear

Not all animals in the war fit standard roles. Some became famous for their unusual duties, blurring the line between mascot and working animal. One of the most well-known examples is Wojtek the bear, who served with Polish forces during the war. Wojtek was found as a cub in Iran by Polish soldiers who had been released from Soviet camps and were making their way to the Middle East. The soldiers adopted him, raising him within their unit. As he grew, Wojtek became part of daily life, eating, playing, and even mimicking human behavior, such as drinking from bottles and carrying objects. During the Italian campaign in 1944, Wojtek's role became more practical. He was trained to carry heavy crates of artillery shells, particularly during the Battle of Monte Cassino. His strength and ability to move across difficult terrain made him useful for transporting supplies under challenging conditions. To officially include him, the Polish unit even enlisted him as a soldier, giving him a rank and service number. Wojtek became a symbol of the unit, appearing on their insignia as a bear carrying a shell. His presence boosted morale and created a sense of identity among the soldiers, especially those who had experienced displacement and hardship before reaching the front. Other unusual animal roles also appeared during the war. Experiments were conducted with dolphins and sea lions for naval detection, while some armies attempted to train animals for sabotage missions, with mixed and often unsuccessful results. These efforts reflected both innovation and desperation, as militaries explored unconventional methods to gain an advantage. The story of Wojtek, however, stands out for a different reason. He wasn't just a tool of war but a companion who shared the experience of the soldiers around him. His story highlights how, even in the most mechanized conflict in history, animals remained a part of the human experience of war.

EIGHT

Daily Life In World War II

For civilians, World War II transformed everyday life in profound ways. The war reached into homes, workplaces, and communities, reshaping routines and expectations. Rationing, blackouts, and constant uncertainty became part of daily existence, while governments mobilized entire populations to support the war effort. This chapter explores life on the home front, including the social and economic changes brought about by the conflict. It looks at how ordinary people adapted to extraordinary circumstances, balancing fear, responsibility, and the need to continue living under the pressures of war. It was a time when the line between civilian and combatant blurred, and survival required resilience far from the battlefield.

234. The First Changes: Queues, Coupons, and Quiet Fear

When war was declared in September 1939, daily life didn't collapse overnight, but it changed immediately in subtle and visible ways. In Britain, France, and Germany, governments moved quickly to control food supplies, anticipating shortages long before they fully appeared. Rationing systems were introduced or prepared, requiring civilians to register with local shops and receive ration books filled with coupons. These coupons limited how much sugar, butter, meat, and fuel a person could buy each week. Even before strict rationing fully took effect, people began queuing outside shops, uncertain how long supplies would last. In Britain, for example, rationing officially began in January 1940, but people were already stockpiling goods such as canned food, tea, and flour by late 1939. Long lines formed outside grocers and butchers, and shop shelves could empty quickly after deliveries arrived. In Germany, the government had already begun managing food supplies years earlier, preparing the population for a controlled wartime economy. Citizens were expected to accept limits as part of their duty to the state. Clothing also began to change. New production shifted toward military needs, meaning civilian goods became harder to find. People were encouraged to repair old clothes rather than replace them. Shoes, in particular, became valuable, as leather was increasingly reserved for the military. Despite these changes, much of daily life still continued. People went to work, children attended school, and shops remained open. However, there was an underlying sense of uncertainty. The war had begun, but for most civilians, it was still distant. The real impact had not yet arrived, but the first signs were already visible in ration books, queues, and the quiet awareness that normal life would not last.

235. Blackouts and the Transformation of the Night

One of the first major changes to civilian life was the introduction of blackout regulations. Beginning in 1939, cities across Britain and later other European countries were required to eliminate all visible light at night to make it harder for enemy aircraft to locate targets. This transformed daily routines in ways that were immediate and unavoidable. Streetlights were turned off or heavily dimmed. Windows had to be covered with thick curtains or blackout fabric so that no light could escape. Even a small crack of light could result in fines or warnings from local authorities. Cars were required to use covered headlights that allowed only narrow beams to shine downward, making driving slow and dangerous. Public transport continued, but movement at night became more difficult and disorienting. For civilians, the blackout made ordinary activities more complicated. Walking through the streets after dark became hazardous, with many people stumbling, falling, or getting lost. Accidents increased sharply. In Britain alone, thousands of injuries and deaths were attributed to blackout conditions, including traffic accidents and falls. Inside homes, the blackout changed the rhythm of daily life. Families gathered in single rooms with covered lamps, often going to bed earlier than before. Social life was reduced, and evenings became quieter. The absence of visible light created a constant reminder of the threat from above, even before large-scale bombing began. The blackout wasn't just a safety measure; it was a psychological shift. It marked the moment when civilians understood that the war could reach them directly. Darkness became part of daily life, and with it came a growing awareness that the boundaries between the front line and the home front were beginning to disappear.

236. Evacuation, Separation, and Families Divided

As the threat of bombing increased in 1940, particularly in Britain, governments began large-scale evacuation programs to protect civilians, especially children, from expected air attacks. This led to one of the most emotional and disruptive changes in daily life: the separation of families. In Britain, "Operation Pied Piper" began in September 1939, evacuating over 1.5 million people, mostly children, from cities like London, Birmingham, and Liverpool to rural areas. Children were often sent away with labels attached to their coats, carrying small bags with clothing, gas masks, and ration books. Many were accompanied by teachers or strangers rather than their parents. The experience varied widely. Some children were welcomed into rural homes and treated kindly. Others faced difficult conditions, living with families who resented the burden or treated them as unpaid labor. Many children experienced homesickness, fear, and confusion, having been separated suddenly from their families. Parents who remained in cities lived with constant anxiety, unsure of when they would see their children again. Letters became the main form of contact, but delays and uncertainty made communication difficult. Some families were reunited quickly when early bombing didn't meet expectations, while others remained separated for years. Evacuation changed the structure of family life. Homes were left half-empty, schools were disrupted, and communities were divided between those who left and those who stayed. For many civilians, the war was no longer something distant. It had already altered the most basic relationships, separating parents from children and turning everyday life into something unfamiliar.

237. Air Raids, Sirens, and Living Under Bombardment

By 1940, the war reached civilians directly as large-scale bombing campaigns began, most notably during the Blitz in Britain between September 1940 and May 1941. Daily life became structured around the possibility of air raids, which could begin at any time, often at night. The warning system became part of everyday routine. Air raid sirens signaled incoming aircraft with a rising and falling wail, sending people rushing to shelters. These shelters varied. Some families had small backyard shelters, such as the Anderson shelter, made of corrugated steel and partially buried in the ground. Others relied on public shelters or underground stations, including the London Underground, where thousands of people slept on platforms during bombing raids. Nights were often interrupted by explosions, anti-aircraft fire, and the constant noise of aircraft overhead. Sleep became irregular, and exhaustion was common. Families sometimes spent entire nights in shelters, returning to damaged homes in the morning. Daily routines had to continue despite this. People went to work, children attended school, and services continued to operate even after heavy bombing. However, the threat was always present. Buildings could be destroyed overnight, streets could change completely, and familiar places could disappear. The psychological impact was significant. Civilians lived in fear that they could be targeted without warning. The distinction between soldier and civilian became blurred. Survival depended not on training or weapons, but on luck, timing, and the ability to endure repeated disruption.

238. Rationing Deepens and the Rise of Substitutes

By 1941, the war had expanded, and supply shortages became more severe. Rationing systems tightened across Europe, and civilians had to adapt to living on limited, often poor-quality food. What people ate began to change significantly, shaped by availability rather than preference. In Britain, rationing expanded to include meat, butter, sugar, cheese, and eggs. Weekly allowances were strictly limited. For example, a person might receive only a few ounces of butter or sugar per week. Eggs were rare, often replaced by powdered eggs imported from overseas. Meat was limited, and cheaper cuts became more common. As shortages increased, substitutes became part of daily life. Coffee was replaced by alternatives made from roasted barley or chicory. Butter was replaced by margarine. In Germany, ersatz (substitute) products were widely used, including synthetic coffee and bread mixed with fillers such as potato or other grains. Cooking habits changed as well. Governments issued recipes to help people make meals from limited ingredients. In Britain, dishes like "Woolton pie," made from vegetables rather than meat, became common. People learned to stretch small amounts of food across multiple meals. Food became more than just nutrition. It was a daily challenge. Planning meals required careful use of ration coupons, and shortages couldn't always be avoided. The experience of eating changed from choice to necessity, with civilians adapting to whatever was available.

239. Cold Homes, Fuel Shortages, and Improvised Heating

By 1942, shortages were no longer limited to food. Fuel, coal, wood, and oil became increasingly scarce across both Allied and Axis countries, forcing civilians to rethink how they heated their homes. Governments prioritized fuel for factories, railways, and the military, leaving ordinary households with reduced allocations. In Britain, coal was rationed, and many families were limited to heating only one room in the house during winter. This "living room" became the center of daily life, where families ate, worked, and slept together to conserve warmth. Bedrooms were often left unheated, and people went to bed wearing multiple layers of clothing, sometimes including coats, hats, and gloves. In Germany and occupied Europe, the situation could be even harsher. Bombing had disrupted supply lines, and coal shortages became severe, especially in cities. Civilians burned whatever they could find: broken furniture, wooden fences, books, and even floorboards. Public buildings and schools were sometimes closed during the coldest periods because they couldn't be heated. Improvised solutions became common. People sealed windows with paper or cloth to reduce drafts. Blankets were hung over doorways to trap heat. Hot water bottles, when available, became essential for surviving cold nights. The cold wasn't just uncomfortable; it affected health, especially among the elderly and children. Illnesses increased, and for many, winter became one of the hardest periods of the war. Survival depended not only on avoiding bombs but also on enduring the long, cold months with limited resources.

240. Transport, Bicycles, and the Slowing of Everyday Movement

As fuel shortages worsened in 1942, transportation systems began to change dramatically. Petrol (gasoline) was heavily rationed or reserved entirely for military use, meaning that civilian travel became limited, slower, and often more difficult. Private car use nearly disappeared in many countries. In Britain, most civilian cars were taken off the road, either because fuel was unavailable or because vehicles were requisitioned for military purposes. Public transportation, such as buses and trains, continued to operate but was often overcrowded, unreliable, and subject to delays caused by military priorities. Bicycles became one of the most important forms of transport. Across Europe, people relied on them for commuting, carrying goods, and traveling between towns. In countries like the Netherlands, Denmark, and France, bicycles were already common, but during the war, they became essential. People adapted them creatively, adding baskets, trailers, or wooden platforms to carry food, firewood, or supplies. In occupied areas, movement was often restricted by checkpoints and regulations. Civilians needed permits to travel between regions, and railways were closely controlled. Journeys that once took hours could take an entire day or might not be possible at all. Even small trips required planning. Visiting relatives, going to work, or accessing markets became more complicated. Distance felt larger, and everyday movement slowed down. The war reshaped not just what people did, but how they moved through their world, turning simple travel into a challenge.

241. Clothing Shortages and the Culture of Repair

By 1942 and into 1943, clothing became another major area of shortage. Textile production had shifted toward military uniforms, parachutes, and equipment, leaving fewer resources for civilian clothing. Governments introduced rationing systems to control the use of fabric and ensure fair distribution. In Britain, clothing was rationed using coupons, similar to food. Each person received a limited number of coupons per year, which had to be used carefully. A new coat or pair of shoes could consume a large portion of a person's allowance, meaning that most people avoided buying new items unless absolutely necessary. As a result, repair and reuse became part of daily life. Clothes were patched, altered, and reused as long as possible. Old garments were taken apart and remade into new ones. Children's clothes were passed down between siblings, often modified to fit. Women were encouraged to "make do and mend," a phrase used in government campaigns to promote conservation. Materials also changed. Synthetic fabrics and lower-quality materials were used more frequently. Some clothing was made from unusual sources, including repurposed curtains or blankets. Shoes, in particular, became difficult to replace, leading people to repair soles repeatedly or wear damaged footwear. Appearance shifted as well. Fashion became simpler, more practical, and less varied. Bright colors and decorative elements were less common, replaced by functional designs. Clothing reflected the reality of wartime life: limited, practical, and often worn.

242. Hygiene, Water Shortages, and Everyday Improvisation

As the war continued, maintaining personal hygiene became increasingly difficult, especially in heavily bombed or occupied areas. Water supplies were often disrupted by damaged infrastructure, and soap and cleaning products became scarce. Bathing became less frequent. In many places, people relied on public bathhouses, which operated on limited schedules and were often crowded. At home, families used small amounts of water for washing, sometimes heating it manually and sharing it among multiple people. Soap was rationed or difficult to obtain. In some countries, it was replaced with lower-quality substitutes that were less effective. People improvised, using whatever was available to stay clean. Clothes were washed less often, and maintaining cleanliness required effort and creativity. Hair and grooming also changed. Women often cut their hair shorter to make it easier to manage without regular washing. Men shaved less frequently when razors and blades were scarce. Personal appearance became secondary to practicality. Despite these challenges, hygiene remained important for health. Poor sanitation could lead to illness, especially in crowded urban areas or shelters. People developed routines to manage with limited resources, showing how even basic activities required adaptation during the war.

243. Boredom, Waiting, and the Rhythm of War

Not every moment of civilian life was filled with danger. Much of wartime life was defined by waiting, uncertainty, and long periods of boredom. The pace of daily life slowed, shaped by shortages, restrictions, and limited entertainment. Work continued for many, especially in factories, offices, and farms. However, outside of work, options were reduced. Travel was limited, entertainment venues were restricted or closed, and curfews were sometimes imposed. Evenings were often quiet, especially during blackout conditions. People found ways to fill the time. Reading, knitting, and listening to the radio became common activities. Radios were an important source of news and entertainment, broadcasting music, speeches, and updates from the front. However, in occupied territories, listening to foreign broadcasts could be dangerous or illegal. Community activities also played a role. Neighbors gathered to share news, help each other, or simply talk. Small routines, cooking, repairing, and cleaning provided structure to days that might otherwise feel uncertain. At the same time, waiting carried emotional weight. People waited for news from the front, for letters from loved ones, and for signs that the war might end. This waiting was often filled with anxiety, as information was limited and outcomes were unclear. The war wasn't only experienced in moments of crisis. It was also lived in the spaces between, in the long, quiet periods when uncertainty became part of everyday life.

244. Black Markets, Barter, and the Shadow Economy

By 1943, official rationing systems in many countries could no longer meet the needs of civilians. As shortages worsened, a parallel economy emerged: the black market. This underground system became essential for survival, even though it was illegal and often harshly punished. In Germany, France, Italy, and other parts of occupied Europe, ration cards provided only minimal food. Meat, butter, eggs, and sugar were often unavailable through official channels. As a result, people turned to unofficial sources, buying food directly from farmers or traders willing to operate outside government control. Barter became common. Instead of money, people exchanged goods. Clothing, jewelry, cigarettes, and even family heirlooms were traded for food. In cities, civilians would travel to the countryside carrying suitcases of items to exchange for bread, potatoes, or meat. These journeys were risky, as authorities often tried to prevent unauthorized trade. Prices on the black market were high, often far beyond what ordinary people could afford. This created inequality. Those with valuable items or connections could access better food, while others relied on official rations and went hungry. Despite the risks, the black market became a normal part of life. For many civilians, it wasn't a matter of choice but necessity. Survival increasingly depended not on official systems but on informal networks, negotiation, and luck.

245. Bombing Intensifies and the Destruction of Cities

By 1943, the scale of bombing in Europe had increased dramatically. Allied air forces began sustained bombing campaigns against German cities, while German bombing had earlier targeted cities like London. Civilians found themselves living under constant threat from the air. In Germany, cities such as Hamburg experienced devastating air raids. In July 1943, bombing created a firestorm, where intense heat and wind combined to produce fires that spread uncontrollably. Entire neighborhoods were destroyed, and tens of thousands of people were killed in a matter of days. Daily life became organized around the expectation of air raids. Sirens warned of incoming aircraft, giving civilians time to move to shelters. People slept in basements, bunkers, or public shelters, often crowded with neighbors. Nights were frequently interrupted, leaving people exhausted. Buildings were damaged or destroyed, leaving many homeless. Families were forced to move repeatedly, staying with relatives or in temporary housing. Streets were filled with rubble, and essential services such as water, electricity, and transport were often disrupted. Children were sometimes evacuated from cities to safer rural areas. In Britain, this process had begun earlier, but similar evacuations occurred in Germany later in the war. Families were separated for long periods, adding emotional strain to physical danger. Bombing changed the nature of civilian life. The home, once a place of safety, became a potential target.

246. Displacement, Refugees, and the Movement of Civilians

By 1944, the war was no longer confined to distant fronts. As armies advanced across Europe, millions of civilians were forced to move, either to escape fighting or because they were ordered to evacuate. In Eastern Europe, entire communities fled ahead of advancing armies. Civilians traveled on foot, by cart, or by overcrowded trains, carrying only what they could take with them. These journeys were often chaotic, with limited food, shelter, or protection. In Western Europe, the Allied invasion of Normandy in June 1944 brought fighting directly into towns and villages. Civilians were caught between armies, forced to leave their homes or shelter in place as battles took place around them. Cities damaged by bombing became difficult to live in. Housing shortages forced people into crowded conditions, sometimes sharing space with strangers. Public buildings, schools, and churches were used as temporary shelters. Refugees faced constant uncertainty. They often didn't know where they were going, how long they would be gone, or whether they would be able to return home. Families were sometimes separated during these movements, adding to the confusion and stress. The war created a large population of displaced people, individuals who were no longer connected to a stable place of living. Movement became a defining feature of civilian life, as millions searched for safety in a landscape shaped by conflict.

247. Hunger, Collapse, and the Limits of Survival

As the war approached its final phase, conditions in many areas deteriorated further. Supply systems broke down, infrastructure was destroyed, and food became increasingly difficult to obtain. In parts of Europe, especially in areas affected by fighting or occupation, hunger reached severe levels. One example is the Dutch "Hunger Winter" of 1944–1945, when food shortages in the Netherlands led to widespread malnutrition and starvation. People ate whatever they could find, including tulip bulbs and animal feed, to survive. In Germany, constant bombing and disrupted transport made it difficult to distribute food. Rations decreased, and shortages became more severe. Cities struggled to maintain basic services, and everyday life became increasingly unstable. Fuel shortages worsened as well, making heating and cooking difficult. Many homes were damaged or destroyed, leaving people exposed to the elements. Winter conditions added to the hardship. The collapse of systems meant that survival depended on individual resourcefulness. People relied on remaining supplies, local networks, and whatever could be improvised. The structures that had once supported daily life, transport, distribution, and administration were no longer reliable. By this stage of the war, civilian life was defined by endurance. The focus shifted from adaptation to survival as people faced the final, most difficult months of the conflict.

248. Liberation, Ruins, and the Return to Uncertainty

When the war in Europe ended in 1945, civilian life didn't return to normal immediately. Instead, many people found themselves in cities that had been heavily damaged or destroyed, with limited resources and uncertain futures. Buildings lay in ruins, and infrastructure such as roads, railways, and utilities needed to be rebuilt. Many people were homeless, living in temporary shelters or damaged buildings. Food shortages continued, and rationing remained in place in many countries even after the fighting ended. At the same time, liberation brought relief. Occupied territories were freed, and restrictions imposed by occupying forces were lifted. People who had lived under control or fear began to rebuild their lives. Families attempted to reunite, but not all were able to do so. Many people had been displaced, captured, or killed, and the process of finding loved ones could take months or years. The end of the war marked a transition rather than a resolution. While the fighting had stopped, the effects of years of conflict remained visible in cities, communities, and individuals. Civilian life moved from survival in wartime to the challenges of rebuilding in peace.

NINE

Atrocities and Occupation

World War II was marked not only by combat but also by acts of violence and oppression carried out against civilian populations. Occupied territories faced harsh control, forced labor, and systematic persecution, while millions suffered under policies that led to widespread suffering and loss of life. This chapter examines the realities of occupation and the atrocities committed during the war, including the treatment of prisoners, the impact on civilian populations, and the systems of control imposed by occupying forces. It also considers the responses of those who resisted, collaborated, or struggled to survive. It was a conflict that revealed the darkest aspects of human behavior, leaving scars that would endure long after the fighting ended.

249. The Invasion of Poland and the Systematic Targeting of Civilians

When Germany invaded Poland in September 1939, violence against civilians began immediately alongside military operations. German forces carried out executions aimed at eliminating Polish leadership, intellectuals, and professionals in an operation later known as the Intelligenzaktion. By the end of 1939, an estimated 50,000–60,000 Polish elites had been killed. Entire communities were subjected to arrests, forced removals, and executions. Villages suspected of resistance were destroyed, and civilians were often shot in reprisal for attacks on German troops. At the same time, Nazi racial policies began to reshape the country. Polish Jews, numbering over three million people, faced immediate restrictions, including forced labor, property confiscation, and segregation. Poland was divided between Germany and the Soviet Union. In the Soviet-controlled east, mass deportations took place, with hundreds of thousands of people sent to labor camps. One of the most notable crimes was the Katyn massacre (1940), where approximately 22,000 Polish officers and officials were executed by Soviet forces. From the beginning, occupation meant not just control of territory but the deliberate dismantling of society.

250. Ghettos and the Systematic Isolation of Jewish Communities

As Nazi control expanded in Eastern Europe, Jewish populations were forced into segregated urban districts known as ghettos. Beginning in 1940, cities such as Warsaw, Łódź, and Kraków saw entire neighborhoods sealed off with walls, fences, and guarded entrances. The Warsaw Ghetto, the largest, confined over 400,000 people into an area of just 1.3 square miles (about 3.4 square kilometers). Conditions inside ghettos were severe. Overcrowding was extreme, with multiple families often sharing single rooms. Food rations were set far below subsistence levels; in some cases, official allocations provided as little as 200–300 calories per day. Starvation became widespread, and disease spread quickly due to poor sanitation and lack of medical care. Typhus outbreaks were common. Despite these conditions, daily life continued in limited ways. Schools operated secretly, and informal economies developed as people traded goods to survive. Smuggling, especially by children, became essential to bring in food at great personal risk. Many were caught and shot. The ghettos weren't intended as permanent settlements. They were part of a larger system of control that isolated Jewish communities, making them easier to exploit and, later, to deport.

251. The Invasion of the Soviet Union and Mass Shootings by Einsatzgruppen

When Germany launched Operation Barbarossa in June 1941, the war in the East quickly became one of unprecedented brutality. Following the advancing German army were special SS (*Schutzstaffel*, or "Protection Squadron") units known as *Einsatzgruppen*, tasked with eliminating perceived enemies of the Reich, particularly Jewish communities, political officials, and intellectuals. Unlike later camps, the killings in 1941 were carried out in open spaces, forests, ravines, and fields. Victims were often gathered under false pretenses, told they were being relocated or registered. They were then taken to isolated areas, forced to dig or stand near mass graves, and shot in large groups. Local collaborators were sometimes involved in identifying or guarding victims. One of the most well-known massacres occurred at Babi Yar, near Kyiv, in September 1941, in which over 33,000 Jews were killed in two days. Across Eastern Europe, similar actions took place repeatedly, resulting in the deaths of more than one million people in what historians later described as the "Holocaust by bullets." These killings also affected those carrying them out. Some German soldiers reported psychological strain, leading commanders to seek more "efficient" methods of mass murder. The experience of 1941 would directly influence the later development of industrialized killing systems in camps.

252. The Siege of Leningrad and Civilian Starvation as a Weapon of War

In September 1941, German and Finnish forces surrounded the Soviet city of Leningrad (modern St. Petersburg), beginning a siege that would last 872 days. Rather than storm the city, the German strategy focused on cutting it off completely, preventing food, fuel, and supplies from entering. The aim wasn't only military defeat but also the collapse of the civilian population through starvation. By the winter of 1941–1942, conditions inside the city had become catastrophic. Food rations dropped to as little as 4.4 ounces (about 125 grams) of bread per day, often mixed with sawdust or other substitutes. Fuel shortages meant that homes couldn't be heated, and temperatures fell far below freezing. Water systems failed, forcing civilians to collect ice or water from frozen rivers. Hunger became the central reality of daily life. People collapsed in the streets, too weak to move. Bodies were often left where they fell because families lacked the strength to bury them. Reports of cannibalism, though rare, were documented as desperation grew. Despite these conditions, the city didn't surrender. Civilians continued to work in factories, maintain defenses, and transport supplies across the frozen "Road of Life" on Lake Ladoga. By the time the siege was lifted in 1944, over one million civilians had died, making it one of the deadliest sieges in history.

253. From Mass Shootings to Industrialized Killing

In the early years of the war, Nazi Germany's persecution of Jews and other targeted groups relied heavily on mass shootings carried out by mobile killing units known as *Einsatzgruppen*. However, these methods were seen by Nazi leadership as inefficient and psychologically difficult for those carrying them out. By late 1941, plans were underway to create a more centralized system of killing. This shift was formalized in January 1942 at the Wannsee Conference, where officials coordinated what they called the "Final Solution," the plan to systematically eliminate Europe's Jewish population. This marked a turning point in the Holocaust. Killing was no longer carried out mainly in open spaces but was reorganized into a system designed for scale, secrecy, and efficiency. The focus moved from localized massacres to a coordinated effort across occupied Europe, laying the foundation for the extermination camps that would soon follow.

254. Extermination Camps and the Systematic Murder of Millions

Beginning in 1942, Nazi Germany established a network of extermination camps in occupied Poland, including Auschwitz-Birkenau, Treblinka, Sobibor, and Belzec. Unlike concentration camps, which were used for imprisonment and forced labor, these facilities were designed specifically for mass killing. Victims were transported to the camps in sealed freight trains from across Europe. These journeys could last several days, with little or no food, water, or sanitation, and many died before arrival. Upon reaching the camps, prisoners were subjected to a rapid selection process. Those considered able to work were sent to labor, while the majority, including children, the elderly, and many women, were sent directly to gas chambers. These chambers used gases such as carbon monoxide or Zyklon B to kill large groups at once. The process was organized with a high degree of efficiency. Bodies were removed, valuables were taken, and remains were burned or buried. Personal belongings were sorted and redistributed, often sent back to Germany. Victims were frequently misled about their fate, told they were entering showers or undergoing disinfection. By the end of the war, approximately six million Jews had been murdered, alongside millions of others, including Roma, Soviet prisoners of war, disabled individuals, and political prisoners. The scale, organization, and intent behind these killings made the Holocaust one of the most systematic and devastating acts of mass violence in modern history.

255. Forced Labor Across Occupied Europe

As the war intensified, Nazi Germany faced a growing need for labor to sustain its military and industrial production. To meet this demand, a vast system of forced labor was created across occupied Europe. Millions of civilians were taken from their homes and transported to Germany or forced to work in their own countries under German control. By 1944, an estimated seven to eight million foreign laborers were working within the

German economy. In Western Europe, workers were often recruited through pressure or deception, but as the war continued, forced conscription became more common. In France, the Service du Travail Obligatoire (STO) required young men to work in German factories. In Eastern Europe, the system was far harsher. Civilians, including teenagers, were seized in raids and transported under guard. These workers, often referred to as *Ostarbeiter* (Eastern workers), faced strict controls, poor living conditions, and limited rights. Workers were housed in overcrowded camps or barracks, received minimal food, and were subject to strict discipline. Movement was restricted, and contact with local populations was often forbidden. Many were forced to work long hours in factories producing weapons, vehicles, and other military supplies. Resistance or attempts to escape could result in severe punishment or execution. Forced labor became a central part of the German war effort, linking occupation policies directly to industrial production. It demonstrated how civilian populations were exploited on a massive scale, turning human lives into resources for sustaining the war.

256. Reprisals, Partisans, and the Violence of Occupation

As resistance movements grew across occupied Europe, German forces responded with increasingly harsh reprisals against civilian populations. Partisan groups operated in countries such as Yugoslavia, Poland, Greece, and the Soviet Union, carrying out sabotage, ambushes, and intelligence gathering. These actions disrupted German control but also led to severe consequences for civilians. Occupation authorities often applied collective punishment, targeting entire communities for the actions of a few. Villages suspected of supporting resistance were burned, and inhabitants were executed or deported. In some areas, German policy followed strict ratios; for every German soldier killed, dozens or even hundreds of civilians could be executed in retaliation. Several massacres became widely known. In 1942, the Czech village of Lidice was destroyed after the assassination of Reinhard Heydrich. All men were executed, women deported, and children either killed or sent to German families for "re-education." In France, the village of Oradour-sur-Glane was destroyed in 1944, with over 600 civilians killed. These reprisals were intended to discourage resistance but often had the opposite effect, strengthening opposition and increasing support for partisan groups. For civilians, the line between battlefield and home disappeared. Everyday life was shaped by the constant risk that violence could occur without warning, making occupation a condition of fear and uncertainty.

257. The Liquidation of Ghettos and Uprisings

By 1943, Nazi policy moved toward the complete liquidation of Jewish ghettos across occupied Eastern Europe. Ghettos that had existed for years as sites of forced labor, starvation, and confinement were systematically emptied. Their populations were deported to extermination camps such as Treblinka and Auschwitz or killed on the spot. This marked a final phase in the destruction of Jewish communities that had once formed a central part of urban life in cities like Warsaw and Łódź. In some ghettos, resistance emerged despite overwhelming odds. The most well-known example was the Warsaw Ghetto Uprising in April 1943. When German forces entered to carry out deportations, Jewish fighters, many armed only with pistols, homemade explosives, and limited ammunition, launched an organized resistance. For nearly a month, they fought German troops using the narrow streets, buildings, and underground passages of the ghetto. The uprising was eventually crushed. German forces systematically destroyed the area, burning buildings and using heavy weapons to eliminate resistance. Approximately 13,000 Jews were killed during the fighting, and tens of thousands more were deported to camps. The ghetto was left in ruins. Although militarily unsuccessful, such uprisings demonstrated that resistance existed even in the most extreme conditions. They became symbols of defiance, showing that even in a system designed to eliminate entire populations, some chose to resist despite knowing the likely outcome.

258. Bombing Campaigns and the Destruction of Cities

As the war progressed, large-scale bombing campaigns became a central part of strategy, bringing the war directly into civilian areas. Both the Allies and Axis powers targeted cities to disrupt industry, transport, and morale. Bombing raids increasingly focused on urban centers, where factories and civilian populations were concentrated. In Germany, cities such as Hamburg, Cologne, and Dresden were heavily bombed. One of the most destructive raids occurred in Hamburg in July 1943 during Operation Gomorrah. A combination of high-explosive and incendiary bombs created a firestorm, where intense heat generated hurricane-like winds that fed the flames. Entire neighborhoods were destroyed, and approximately 40,000 people were killed in a matter of days. Bombing campaigns blurred the line between military and civilian targets. While factories and transport networks were primary objectives, residential areas were often affected, leading to large numbers of civilian casualties. People lived with the constant threat of air raids, spending nights in shelters, basements, or underground stations. The destruction of cities changed the nature of the war.

259. Death Marches and the Collapse of the Camp System

As Allied forces advanced into German-occupied territories in 1944 and 1945, the Nazi regime began evacuating concentration and extermination camps in an attempt to prevent prisoners from being liberated. Tens of thousands of prisoners were forced onto long marches toward the interior of Germany in what became known as "death marches." These marches took place in extreme conditions, often during winter, with little food, water, or rest. Prisoners, already weakened by starvation, disease, and forced labor, were required to walk long distances under guard. Anyone who fell behind, collapsed, or was unable to continue was often shot on the spot. The routes were chaotic and poorly organized. Columns of prisoners moved along roads crowded with refugees, retreating troops, and collapsing infrastructure. In some cases, trains were used, but these were often overcrowded and lacked basic necessities, leading to further deaths. It is estimated that tens of thousands of prisoners died during these evacuations. The marches revealed the extent of brutality within the camp system, even as it was collapsing. Rather than abandon the camps, authorities chose to move prisoners under conditions that ensured many would not survive. For those who did survive, liberation often came shortly afterward, as Allied forces reached the camps and encountered the remaining prisoners and evidence of the system that had operated across occupied Europe.

260. The Firebombing of Cities and the Destruction of Urban Life

As the war entered its final phase, aerial bombing intensified to unprecedented levels, turning entire cities into targets. Allied bombing campaigns aimed not only at military and industrial sites but also at breaking the enemy's ability to sustain war. One of the most devastating attacks occurred in Hamburg in July 1943 (Operation Gomorrah), where firestorms created by incendiary bombs killed an estimated 37,000 people. By 1944–1945, similar tactics were used repeatedly across German cities. The bombing of Dresden in February 1945 became one of the most controversial events. Over several days, waves of British and American bombers dropped high-explosive and incendiary bombs, creating a firestorm that destroyed much of the city. Estimates of the death toll vary, but tens of thousands of civilians were killed. In Japan, the scale of destruction was equally severe. The firebombing of Tokyo on the night of March 9–10, 1945, killed an estimated 80,000–100,000 people in a single raid, making it one of the deadliest air attacks in history. The city, largely built of wood, burned rapidly, and many victims died from fire or suffocation. For civilians, bombing transformed daily life into a constant state of fear. Air raid sirens, shelters, and blackout routines became part of survival. Cities that had once been centers of life were reduced to ruins, showing how modern warfare extended destruction far beyond the battlefield.

261. Hiroshima and the First Atomic Bomb

On August 6, 1945, the United States dropped the first atomic bomb used in warfare on the Japanese city of Hiroshima. The bomb, code-named *Little Boy*, was released from the B-29 bomber *Enola Gay* and detonated approximately 1,968 feet (600 meters) above the city. In a matter of seconds, an immense explosion and flash of heat destroyed much of Hiroshima. Temperatures at the center of the blast reached several thousand degrees Fahrenheit, with some estimates exceeding 7,000 degrees Fahrenheit (3,900 degrees Celsius), igniting fires across the city and vaporizing buildings and people close to the impact point. An estimated 70,000–80,000 people were killed instantly. Many victims died from the blast itself, while others were burned by the intense heat or crushed by collapsing structures. In the days and weeks that followed, tens of thousands more died from severe injuries and radiation exposure. Survivors often suffered burns, blindness, and radiation sickness, with symptoms including nausea, hair loss, and internal bleeding. The destruction of Hiroshima demonstrated a new level of warfare. Unlike conventional bombing, a single weapon could destroy an entire city. The use of the atomic bomb was partly intended to force Japan to surrender quickly, but it also reflected a broader context of escalating violence, including earlier firebombing campaigns that had already devastated Japanese urban areas.

262. Nagasaki, Radiation, and the End of the War

Three days after Hiroshima, on August 9, 1945, a second atomic bomb, code-named *Fat Man*, was dropped on the city of Nagasaki. The original target was Kokura, but poor visibility led the bomber to divert to Nagasaki. The bomb detonated over the city, causing widespread destruction, though the surrounding hills limited the blast compared to Hiroshima. An estimated 40,000–70,000 people were killed by the end of 1945. As in Hiroshima, many deaths weren't immediate. Survivors suffered from burns, injuries, and radiation sickness, which continued to claim lives in the following months and years. Radiation exposure became one of the most defining features of atomic warfare. People who had survived the initial explosion developed long-term illnesses, including cancers and chronic conditions. These survivors became known as *hibakusha*, many of whom faced not only health problems but also social stigma. The atomic bombings occurred alongside other pressures on Japan, including the Soviet Union's entry into the war against Japan on August 8, 1945, and continued conventional bombing. Facing these combined threats, Emperor Hirohito intervened to accept surrender. On August 15, Japan announced its surrender, with formal documents signed on September 2, 1945. The bombings marked the beginning of the nuclear age. They introduced a form of warfare capable of mass destruction on an unprecedented scale, shaping global politics and military strategy for decades to come.

263. Total Loss, Lasting Wounds, and the Invisible Scars of War

By the end of World War II, the scale of human loss was unprecedented. It is estimated that between seventy and eighty-five million people died worldwide, representing roughly three to four percent of the global population at the time. Civilians made up the majority of these deaths, killed not only in combat zones but also through bombing, starvation, disease, forced labor, and systematic murder. The Soviet Union alone lost an estimated twenty-four to twenty-seven million people, while China suffered around fifteen to twenty million deaths. Germany lost approximately six to seven million people, including civilians, and Japan lost around 2.5–3 million. The Holocaust accounted for the murder of approximately six million Jews, alongside millions of other victims, including Roma, disabled individuals, and prisoners of war. Beyond those killed, millions more were permanently injured. Modern warfare, especially the use of artillery, explosives, and mechanized weapons, caused widespread physical trauma. Soldiers and civilians alike lost limbs, suffered severe burns, or were left with long-term disabilities. Advances in battlefield medicine meant that more people survived injuries that would previously have been fatal, but often with lasting consequences. Amputations became common, and many survivors required lifelong care, prosthetics, or assistance. The psychological impact of the war was equally significant, though less visible. What was then referred to as "combat fatigue" or "shell shock" is now recognized as post-traumatic stress disorder. Soldiers who had experienced prolonged exposure to combat often suffered from anxiety, nightmares, emotional numbness, and difficulty returning to civilian life.

Civilians, especially those who endured bombings, occupation, or imprisonment, experienced similar effects. At the time, understanding of these conditions was limited, and many struggled without formal support. The end of the war didn't mark the end of its consequences. Physical injuries, psychological trauma, and the loss of millions of lives continued to shape societies long after the fighting stopped, leaving a legacy that extended far beyond 1945.

TEN

The End & the Long Shadow

The conclusion of World War II marked the end of large-scale fighting, but it did not bring an immediate return to stability. The destruction left behind was immense, and the consequences of the war would continue to shape the world for decades to come. Nations faced the challenge of rebuilding, while new political tensions emerged in the aftermath of the conflict. This chapter explores the final stages of the war and its lasting impact, including the reshaping of borders, the rise of new global powers, and the beginning of a new era defined by both recovery and uncertainty. It highlights how the effects of the war extended far beyond its official end. It was a conclusion that marked not just the end of a conflict but the beginning of a transformed world whose influence continues to be felt today.

264. Germany's Collapse and the Division into Occupation Zones

After Germany's surrender in May 1945, the country ceased to function as a unified state. Its government had collapsed, its cities were heavily damaged, and its infrastructure was in ruins. The Allied powers, the United States, the Soviet Union, Britain, and France, divided Germany into four occupation zones, each controlled by one of the victors. Berlin, although located deep within the Soviet zone, was also divided into four sectors, reflecting the shared control over the former capital. Occupation authorities faced immediate challenges. Millions of soldiers had to be disarmed, prisoners of war processed, and Nazi institutions dismantled.

Denazification programs were introduced to remove former Nazi officials from positions of power, though implementation varied widely between zones. In the Soviet-controlled areas, land reforms and political restructuring began quickly, while in the western zones, efforts focused on rebuilding administrative systems and stabilizing the economy. For civilians, occupation meant uncertainty. Laws changed, currencies lost value, and authority shifted overnight. Food shortages remained severe, and many relied on rationing or black markets to survive. The division of Germany, initially intended as a temporary measure, would later become a central issue in the emerging Cold War, shaping Europe for decades to come.

265. Displaced Persons and the Largest Migration in European History

The end of the war didn't bring immediate stability to millions of people across Europe. Instead, it triggered one of the largest population movements in modern history. By 1945, an estimated thirty to forty million people were displaced, including former prisoners of war, forced laborers, concentration camp survivors, and civilians fleeing advancing armies or destroyed homes. Many of these individuals were referred to as "Displaced Persons" (DPs). Allied authorities established camps to house them temporarily, but conditions were often crowded, and resources were limited. Some people were able to return home, but for others, this was impossible. Borders had shifted, governments had changed, and in some cases, returning meant facing persecution or arrest. One of the largest forced migrations involved ethnic Germans living in Eastern Europe. Between 1945 and 1950, around twelve to fourteen million Germans were expelled or fled from countries such as Poland, Czechoslovakia, and Hungary. These movements were often chaotic and violent, with many dying from exposure, disease, or attacks during the journey. For survivors of the Holocaust, displacement carried an additional burden. Many had lost entire families and communities, with no homes to return to. Some emigrated to countries such as the United States, while others moved to Palestine, contributing to tensions that would later shape the Middle East. The war's end didn't restore stability; for millions, it marked the beginning of another uncertain journey.

266. The Nuremberg Trials and the Question of Justice

After the war, the Allied powers faced a major question: how to deal with the leaders responsible for the conflict and its crimes. Rather than executing them without trial, they chose to establish an international tribunal in the German city of Nuremberg. Beginning in November 1945, leading figures of Nazi Germany were put on trial for crimes against peace (starting the war), war crimes, and crimes against humanity (including mass killings and persecution). Twenty-two major Nazi officials were tried, including Hermann Göring, Joachim von Ribbentrop, and Albert Speer. The trials presented extensive evidence, including documents, films, and witness testimony, revealing the scale of atrocities such as the Holocaust. For many people around the world, this was the first time the full extent of Nazi crimes became widely known. The outcomes varied. Twelve defendants were sentenced to death, others received long prison terms, and a few were acquitted. The trials established an important legal precedent: individuals, including political and military leaders, could be held personally responsible for actions carried out by the state. However, the trials were also controversial. Some critics argued that they represented "victor's justice," since only Axis leaders were prosecuted. Despite this, the Nuremberg Trials marked a turning point in international law, shaping future efforts to address war crimes and human rights violations. They demonstrated an attempt to replace revenge with legal accountability, even in the aftermath of a global conflict.

267. The Occupation of Japan and the Remaking of a Nation

Following Japan's surrender in August 1945, the country came under Allied occupation, led primarily by the United States under General Douglas MacArthur. Unlike Germany, Japan wasn't divided among multiple powers; instead, it remained under a single occupation authority, which allowed for more centralized reforms. The occupation aimed not only to demilitarize Japan but also to transform its political system. The Japanese military was dismantled, war industries were reduced, and a new constitution was introduced in 1947. This constitution included a key provision, Article 9, in which Japan renounced war as a sovereign right and agreed not to maintain traditional military forces. Political reforms also expanded democratic rights. Women were granted the right to vote for the first time, and efforts were made to reduce the power of large industrial and political groups. At the same time, war crimes trials were held in Tokyo, similar to those in Nuremberg, prosecuting Japanese leaders for their role in the war. For ordinary civilians, the occupation years were difficult. Cities had been heavily bombed, food shortages were common, and the economy struggled to recover. However, the reforms laid the foundation for Japan's postwar recovery. Within a decade, the country began to rebuild its economy and political system, eventually becoming one of the world's leading industrial powers. The occupation of Japan showed a different model of postwar reconstruction, focused not only on control but also on long-term transformation.

268. Hiroshima, Nagasaki, and the Long Shadow of Radiation

After the atomic bombings of Hiroshima and Nagasaki, destruction didn't end with the explosions. Survivors, later known as *hibakusha* ("bomb-affected people"), continued to suffer long after the cities were rebuilt. Many experienced severe burns that healed slowly or left permanent scars, known as keloids. Others developed symptoms of radiation sickness, including hair loss, bleeding, fatigue, and weakened immune systems. In the months and years that followed, doctors began to observe higher rates of leukemia and other cancers among survivors. These illnesses often appeared years after exposure, making the long-term effects difficult to fully understand at the time. Children exposed to radiation faced particular risks, and concerns also arose about genetic damage, though research later showed more limited hereditary effects than initially feared. Social consequences were also significant. Many hibakusha faced discrimination, as others feared radiation could be contagious. Survivors often struggled to find employment or marriage partners due to stigma. At the same time, Hiroshima and Nagasaki became symbols of nuclear destruction. Memorials, survivor testimonies, and peace movements grew in the postwar years, shaping global debates about nuclear weapons. The atomic bombings didn't end with 1945; they marked the beginning of a new era in which the effects of war could last across generations.

269. Europe in Ruins and the Struggle to Rebuild

By the end of the war in Europe, much of the continent lay in ruins. Major cities such as Berlin, Warsaw, and Dresden had been heavily bombed or fought over, leaving vast areas destroyed. In Warsaw, for example, around eighty-five percent of the city had been reduced to rubble. Infrastructure, including railways, bridges, and factories, was severely damaged, making transport and production difficult. For civilians, daily life was shaped by shortages. Food, fuel, and basic goods were limited, and rationing continued in many countries well into the late 1940s. In the harsh winter of 1946–1947, often called the "Hunger Winter" in parts of Europe, freezing temperatures and poor harvests worsened conditions. People relied on black markets, barter, or aid from occupying forces and international organizations. Reconstruction required both physical rebuilding and economic support.

270. The "Iron Curtain" and the Division of Europe

In March 1946, former British Prime Minister Winston Churchill delivered a speech in Fulton, Missouri, where he declared that an "Iron Curtain" had descended across Europe. This phrase described the growing division between Western Europe, influenced by the United States and democratic systems, and Eastern Europe, increasingly controlled by the Soviet Union. Although the war had ended less than a year earlier, the alliance between the Western Allies and the Soviet Union was already breaking down. In Eastern Europe, countries such as Poland, Hungary, Romania, and Bulgaria were gradually brought under Soviet influence. Communist parties, often supported by Soviet troops still stationed in the region, took control of governments. Elections were manipulated, opposition parties suppressed, and political systems reshaped along Soviet lines. These states became part of what would later be called the Eastern Bloc. In the West, countries moved toward reconstruction and democratic governance, often supported by American economic aid. The ideological differences between the two sides, capitalism versus communism and democracy versus one-party rule, became more pronounced. Churchill's speech didn't create this division, but it publicly acknowledged it. The wartime alliance had given way to suspicion, competition, and a growing sense that Europe was entering a new kind of conflict, one defined not by direct fighting but by political and ideological rivalry.

271. Decolonization and the Collapse of European Empires

The end of World War II didn't simply reshape Europe; it transformed the global balance of power, accelerating the collapse of European colonial empires. Before the war, countries such as Britain, France, the Netherlands, and Belgium controlled vast territories across Asia, Africa, and the Middle East. However, the war weakened these powers economically and militarily, making it difficult to maintain control over distant colonies. At the same time, the war had changed expectations. Millions of colonial soldiers had fought in the conflict, often in Europe, North Africa, and Asia. They had seen the vulnerability of imperial powers and returned home with new ideas about independence and self-determination. Wartime propaganda, which emphasized freedom and resistance against tyranny, also created contradictions that couldn't easily be ignored by colonized populations. In Asia, independence movements gained momentum quickly. India achieved independence from Britain in 1947, followed by the partition into India and Pakistan, which led to mass migration and violence affecting millions.

In Indonesia, nationalist forces declared independence from the Netherlands in 1945, leading to a four-year conflict before it was recognized in 1949. In Vietnam, resistance against French colonial rule escalated into a prolonged war. In Africa, the process unfolded more gradually, but by the late 1950s and 1960s, many territories were gaining independence. Countries such as Ghana (1957), Algeria (1962), and Kenya (1963) emerged from colonial rule, often after periods of conflict and negotiation. Decolonization wasn't a single event but a global transformation. It reshaped political borders, created new nations, and led to both hope and instability. The legacy of colonial rule, including economic inequality and political tensions, would continue to influence these regions long after independence. In this way, World War II not only ended empires in Europe but also triggered their decline across the world, redefining the international order.

272. The Marshall Plan and the Economic Divide

In June 1947, the United States introduced the European Recovery Program, commonly known as the Marshall Plan, aimed at rebuilding the economies of war-torn Europe. The program provided over $12 billion (more than $100 billion in modern terms) in aid to Western European countries. This assistance included money, raw materials, machinery, and food, helping nations restore industry, rebuild infrastructure, and stabilize their economies. The plan wasn't only economic but also political. American leaders believed that poverty and instability could lead to the spread of communism. By supporting economic recovery, they hoped to strengthen democratic governments and reduce the appeal of Soviet influence. Countries such as France, West Germany, Italy, and the Netherlands benefited significantly, experiencing faster recovery and improved living conditions. The Soviet Union viewed the Marshall Plan as a threat. It rejected the offer of aid and pressured Eastern European countries to do the same. Instead, the Soviet Union established its own system of economic cooperation within the Eastern Bloc. This decision deepened the division of Europe into two separate economic and political spheres. The Marshall Plan contributed to recovery in the West but also solidified the emerging Cold War (1947–1991), a decades-long ideological and geopolitical struggle in which cooperation between former allies was replaced by competition, mistrust, and proxy conflicts.

273. The Berlin Blockade and Airlift

By 1948, Germany had become the central point of tension between the former Allies. As the Western Allies began to rebuild their zones and introduce a new currency to stabilize the economy, the Soviet Union viewed this as a threat to its influence. In June 1948, Soviet forces blocked all road, rail, and canal access to West Berlin, attempting to force the Western Allies out of the city. This blockade cut off more than two million civilians from supplies, including food, fuel, and medicine. Instead of withdrawing, the United States and its allies responded with the Berlin Airlift. For nearly a year, cargo planes flew into West Berlin around the clock, delivering essential goods. At its peak, a plane landed every few minutes. Over 2.3 million tons of supplies were delivered, keeping the city alive through the winter. The operation demonstrated both technological capability and political determination. In May 1949, the Soviet Union lifted the blockade. The crisis marked one of the first major confrontations of the Cold War and showed that while direct war was avoided, the conflict between East and West would continue through pressure, strategy, and symbolic standoffs.

274. The Division of Germany into East and West

Following the Berlin Crisis, the division of Germany became permanent. In May 1949, the Western occupation zones were formally merged to create the Federal Republic of Germany (West Germany), with a democratic government supported by the United States, Britain, and France. In response, the Soviet Union established the German Democratic Republic (East Germany) in October 1949, creating a separate socialist state aligned with Moscow. This division reflected the broader split of Europe. West Germany developed a market-based economy and integrated into Western political and military structures, while East Germany adopted a centrally planned economy under a one-party communist system. Berlin remained divided as well, becoming a focal point of tension between the two blocs. For ordinary Germans, the division meant families separated, different political systems, and limited movement across borders. Over time, this separation would become more rigid, eventually leading to the construction of the Berlin Wall in 1961. The division of Germany symbolized the long-term consequences of World War II. What began as a military occupation evolved into a political boundary that would shape Europe for decades, turning Germany into one of the central front lines of the Cold War.

275. Early Memorials and the First Efforts to Remember

As reconstruction progressed, societies began to create physical memorials to the war. In many countries, these took the form of monuments dedicated to fallen soldiers, resistance fighters, or victims of bombing. These memorials often focused on sacrifice, heroism, and national unity, reflecting how governments wanted the war to be remembered. However, the way the war was remembered varied widely. In Western Europe, emphasis was often placed on resistance and liberation, while collaboration and complicity were less openly discussed. In Eastern Europe, memory was shaped by Soviet influence, highlighting the role of the Red Army and framing the war as a struggle against fascism. Other aspects of the war, including certain atrocities, were downplayed or controlled. The Holocaust, in particular, wasn't immediately central to public memory. While evidence of the camps had been revealed at the end of the war, a broader understanding developed slowly. Many early memorials referred to victims in general terms, without specifically identifying Jewish persecution or other targeted groups. Despite these limitations, the 1950s and 1960s marked the beginning of public remembrance. Cemeteries, monuments, and commemorative ceremonies created spaces where the dead could be acknowledged. These early efforts laid the foundation for later, more detailed and critical engagement with the past.

276. Trials, Testimony, and Confronting the Past

By the 1960s, a new phase of memory began, marked by legal trials and the growing importance of survivor testimony. One of the most significant moments was the trial of Adolf Eichmann in 1961, held in Jerusalem. Eichmann, a key organizer of the deportation of Jews during the Holocaust, was captured in Argentina and brought to trial. For many people around the world, this was the first time they heard detailed, personal accounts of the Holocaust from survivors. The trial was widely broadcast and reported, bringing individual experiences into public awareness. Survivors spoke not only about death and destruction but also about daily life in ghettos and camps, the loss of families, and the struggle to survive. These testimonies challenged earlier narratives that had minimized or generalized the suffering of specific groups. In Germany and other countries, similar processes began. Trials of former officials and collaborators forced societies to confront their own roles in the war. Younger generations, who had grown up after the conflict, began asking questions about what their parents and communities had done. This period marked a turning point. The war was no longer remembered only as a story of victory or defeat. It became a subject of moral examination, where responsibility, guilt, and memory were openly discussed. The past could no longer be ignored, and the voices of survivors became central to understanding what had happened.

277. Memory Culture, Education, and "Never Again"

From the 1970s onward, the memory of World War II became more institutionalized, particularly through education, museums, and public commemorations. The Holocaust, in particular, came to be recognized as a central event in understanding the war. Schools began to teach its history more systematically, and memorial sites such as former concentration camps were preserved and opened to the public. Museums and archives collected documents, photographs, and personal testimonies, ensuring that the experiences of victims were recorded and accessible. Films, literature, and academic research also played a role in shaping how the war was understood by new generations. The phrase "Never Again" became a guiding principle in many countries, reflecting a commitment to prevent similar atrocities in the future. This idea influenced the development of international human rights laws and organizations, including the United Nations' efforts to define and prevent genocide. At the same time, memory remained contested. Different countries emphasized different aspects of the war, and debates continued about responsibility, interpretation, and commemoration. However, the overall trend moved toward greater openness and recognition of the war's human cost. By the end of the 20th century, World War II was no longer just a historical event. It had become a central reference point for discussions about violence, human rights, and the responsibilities of states and individuals. The memory of the war continued to shape global perspectives long after the last battles had been fought.

ELEVEN

Conclusion

World War II is often remembered through its largest events, battles, leaders, and the dates that mark its beginning and end. These provide structure, a way to understand a conflict that stretched across continents and involved millions of people. But as this book has shown, the reality of the war is found just as much in the details.

In the unexpected decisions that changed the course of entire campaigns. In the inventions created under pressure, sometimes saving lives and sometimes destroying them. In the experiences of ordinary people, soldiers, civilians, prisoners, and workers who faced situations few had ever imagined possible.

These moments can be surprising. Some are difficult to believe. Others are deeply unsettling. Yet each reveals something essential about the nature of the war.

World War II was not only fought on battlefields; it reached into homes, hospitals, factories, and laboratories. It relied not only on weapons and strategy but also on endurance, improvisation, and the ability of individuals to adapt under extreme conditions. The facts explored in these pages show how unpredictable the conflict could be. Plans failed. Accidents altered outcomes. Small actions had consequences far beyond their immediate moment. At times, survival depended as much on chance as on skill or preparation. They also show the scale of human suffering.

Behind every statistic were real lives, families separated, communities destroyed, and individuals forced to make impossible choices. The war tested the limits of what people could endure, and it exposed both the best and the worst of human behavior. There were acts of courage and cooperation. There were also acts of cruelty, exploitation, and indifference. Often, these existed side by side. The end of the war brought relief, but it did not erase what had happened.

Many of the technologies developed during the conflict continued to shape the modern world. Political tensions that emerged in its aftermath have influenced decades of global relations. The lessons learned about power, responsibility, and the consequences of unchecked ambition remain relevant today.

The events of World War II are not as distant as they may seem. The systems, alliances, and conflicts that define the present have been shaped, in part, by what took place during those years. Understanding the war means looking beyond the well-known milestones and considering the details that reveal how it was lived.

The facts in this book are not just curiosities or isolated stories. They are reminders of how quickly stability can give way to crisis, of how technology can be used in ways both beneficial and destructive, and of how individual choices, even small ones, can have lasting consequences. Above all, they are reminders of the human dimension of war.

World War II was not inevitable, and its outcomes were not guaranteed. It was shaped by decisions, by circumstances, and by people, each acting within the limits and pressures of their time. To study these facts is not only to learn about the past. It is to better understand the present and to recognize the importance of the choices to be made in the future.

References

College Sidekick. "World Civilization II Study Guide." College Sidekick. Accessed January 21, 2026. https://www.collegesidekick.com/study-guides/atd-tcc-worldciv2

Harry S. Truman Presidential Library & Museum. "World War II Collection." Truman Library. Accessed February 3, 2026. https://www.trumanlibrary.gov/library/personal-papers/world-war-ii-collection

History.com Editors. "World War II History." History.com. Accessed January 28, 2026. https://www.history.com/articles/world-war-ii-history

HistoryNet. "How Were Soldiers Drafted in WW2?" HistoryNet. Accessed February 10, 2026. https://historynet.com/how-were-soldiers-drafted-in-ww2/

Medical Department. "Venereal Disease and Treatment during WW2." Med-Dept.com. Accessed January 19, 2026. https://www.med-dept.com/articles/venereal-disease-and-treatment-during-ww2/

The National WWII Museum. "The End of World War II, 1945." The National WWII Museum. Accessed February 14, 2026. https://www.nationalww2museum.org/war/topics/end-world-war-ii-1945

Penn, Lisha B. *Records of Military Agencies Relating to African Americans from the Post–World War I Period to the Korean War*. Washington, DC: National Archives and Records Administration, 2006.

Yale Law School, Lillian Goldman Law Library. "World War II Documents." The Avalon Project. Accessed January 20, 2026. https://avalon.law.yale.edu/subject_menus/wwii.asp

Bonus!

Thanks for supporting me and purchasing this book! I'd like to send you some freebies. They include:

- The digital version of *500 World War I & II Facts*

- The digital version of *101 Idioms and Phrases*

- The audiobook for my best seller *1144 Random Facts*

Scan the QR code below, enter your email and I'll send you all the files. Happy reading!

Check out my other books!